CRAPALACHIA

a Biography of a Place by
SCOTT McCLANAHAN

TWO DOLLAR RADIO
Books too loud to ignore

TWO DOLLAR RADIO is a family-run outfit founded in 2005 with the mission to reaffirm the cultural and artistic spirit of the publishing industry.

We aim to do this by presenting bold works of literary merit, each book, individually and collectively, providing a sonic progression that we believe to be too loud to ignore.

Author photograph: Sarah McClanahan.
Cover bird-man image: *The Orange Knock Out: political cartoon of John C.L. Fitzpatrick, secretary for mines and treasurer, and the coal strike, 1917, unknown photographer and colourist,* from State Library of New South Wales collection, Australia, Call Number P1 / 583.

Typeset in Garamond, the best font ever.
Printed in the United States of America.
No portion of this book may be copied or reproduced, with the exception of quotes used in critical essays and reviews, without the written permission of the publisher.
Please see the Appendix and Notes section on page 159 for a statement from the Author regarding the imagined elements of this true story.

TWO DOLLAR RADIO
Books too loud to ignore

TwoDollarRadio.com
twodollar@TwoDollarRadio.com

For Sarah

"Historical sense and poetic sense should not, in the end, be contradictory, for if poetry is the little myth we make, history is the big myth we live, and in our living, constantly remake."

—Robert Penn Warren

A SHORT HISTORY OF THE McCLANAHAN FAMILY

There were 13 of them. The children had names that ended in *Y* sounds. That night I couldn't sleep so I got out Grandma's picture books and I learned about my blood and the names that ended in *Y* sounds. There was Betty and there was Annie and there was Stirley and there was Stanley and there was Leslie and there was Gary and there was Larry and there was Terry.

Ruby said: "I like names that end in *Y*."

They all grew up in Danese, WV, eating blackberries for breakfast and eating blackberries for lunch and watching the snow come beneath the door in the wintertime. *Holy shit it's cold.*

There was my Uncle Stanley who I never heard say anything except "sheeeeeeeeeeeeet" and who I saw at the hospital one night talking to this other guy about how the state of West Virginia was making people wear a helmet now if they rode a 4-wheeler. He was all pissed off about it and told the guy: "I mean they're gonna let them bunch of queers get married now, and I can't even ride my 4-wheeler without a helmet on."

I flipped the page of the picture book and there was my Aunt Betty. She came over one day and sat at our table and told us this story about Elgie. She didn't hold back. She told us the story about how he was trying to get his pension from the mines. But before he got it, he had to fight for a couple of months. He finally got a letter that went… *"Dear Mr. McClanahan, we regret to inform you that we're unable to approve you at this time. Please send your response within seven days and we'll schedule another hearing."*

Elgie didn't even say anything.

He just took it down to the outhouse and wiped his ass with it. Then he put it back into the envelope, sealed it up, and sent it back. My Aunt Betty was talking like this was an acceptable thing to do. She was telling this story to her 4-, 5-, 6-year-old and 8-year-old nieces and nephews. This was an acceptable story to tell 8-year-old kids.

We were learning.

There was my Uncle Leslie who was tough as hell. How tough was he? That's what I asked Grandma once. She told me too. She told me about how there was this guy called The Toughest Man in Fayette County and he was this ex-con and beat the hell out of any man who ever messed with him. Leslie and The Toughest Man in Fayette County got into it one day about something. And so Leslie kicked the fuck out of The Toughest Man in Fayette County. It was because The Toughest Man in Fayette County always used vulgar language in front of women.

I asked Ruby, "Well how old was Leslie at the time?"

Ruby was quiet and then she said, "Eleven."

There were cousins too. There was my Cousin Bonnie who had this little boy from this man named Ernie. And Ernie had been in jail and made his living cockfighting. And so I saw them down at Pizza Hut and I looked over at Ernie and he was holding little Paul in his arms and smacking him in the face. SMACK. SMACK. He was smacking him hard. Everybody in the Pizza

Hut was horrified because there was little Paul and he wasn't crying about it. He was laughing.

He was laughing because he loved getting slapped in the face.

BUT STOP!

There is one thing you'll never know about my Uncle Nathan. You'll never know just how sweet he was. You'll never know how alive he was.

Then I looked at pictures of my uncles like Uncle G. My Uncle G. was always trying to kill himself, but something always went wrong. One time he was working in a factory up north and living on Lake Erie. He bought a boat and a shotgun and some shells and decided to go out on the boat on a Saturday morning and end his life. He said goodbye to all of his friends and he told his wife it was the end. He had enough guts now. He wanted people to know this time he was truly going to make it happen. So he cleaned the shotgun and went out in his boat. He shined the boat up the day before. He cranked the motor and went out into the middle of the lake. He sat and looked out over the shining water and thought about his life. He knew this was the end. He clicked off the safety, put the barrel in his mouth and pulled the trigger. Nothing happened. He was still alive.

He cracked open the shotgun and he saw it wasn't loaded. When he cleaned it earlier, he took out the shells. He left the shells on the bed. *Shit.*

He took his boat back home and he knew things were different now. He never tried to take his life again.

There were stories about little boys getting ear infections, and

Ruby not having enough money to take them to the doctors. So they just twisted and turned and flipped and flopped in their sick beds crying for days until their eardrums popped *poof* and they eventually went deaf. *What did you say?*

My dad was working at Kroger when he was 19 years old, and one day in a store meeting, the manager was saying the names of these guys who broke into the store and stole a bunch of shit. He said the name of one of the robbers: "Stanley McClanahan."

Then he asked my dad, not thinking. "Do you know him, Mack?"

My dad said: "Yeah, he's my brother."

So the room grew quiet and the manager later apologized to him.

There was my Uncle Grover who suffered from depression and schizophrenia. And instead of taking him to the doctor they brought in a faith healer and had someone hold him down and tried exorcising his demons. This was the way it was done. DEMONS. There was a picture of Elgie's family I found—all eleven of them lined up in a row and so I asked my grandma, "Well who's that and who's this?"

She said—"That's so and so and she killed herself."

Then I said, "Well who's this and who's that?"

Ruby said, "Oh that's so and so—she killed herself."

And out of the 11 children, 5 of them committed suicide.

And so I asked, "Well what happened to Elgie's father?"

She said: "Oh one day he was rocking a baby in his lap and then he put the baby down and went out behind the Johnny house." Then she whispered so Nathan couldn't hear: "And then he shot himself."

I flipped through the picture book and I saw it all. Some of them stayed and had children and some of them went to other places. Some went north to places like Flint, Michigan, and Cleveland, Ohio, and worked in factories. And some worked for General Motors in Flint, Michigan, and some worked in steel mills in Cleveland, Ohio. And the girls went to Washington, DC, and worked as secretaries. And some stayed and became convicted felons, and one married a school teacher named Audrey Karen and had a baby named Scott. And some married wives from faraway places with different accents and had children with different accents too. And so they went to faraway places like San Francisco, California, and Washington, DC, and Richmond, VA. And New York City, NY. And they never saw one another and they did what everyone does, they started living the same old boring fucking story. It's a story full of death and dying, living and life, tits and ass and balls and dicks and pussy. It's an old, old, old story that always begins—they begat and they begat and they begat.

Now a million crazy babies explode from our smiles and start running all over the world so wild and screaming, Ahhhhhhhhhhhhhhhhhhhhhhhhhhhhhhhhhhhhhhhhhhhhhhhh hhhhhhhhhhhhhhhhhhhhhhhhhhhhhhhhhhhhhhhhhhhhhhhh hhhhhhhhhhhhhhhhhhhhhhhhhhhhhhhhhhhhhhhhhhhhhhhh hhhhhhhhhhhhhhhhhhhhhhhhhhhhhhhhhhhhhhhhhhhhhhhh hhhhhhhhhhhhhhhhhhhhhhhhhhhhhhhhhhhhhhhhhhhhh!

SHIT!

A STORY ABOUT RUBY THAT WILL SHED LIGHT ON HER CHARACTER

I didn't want to see her after the operation, but she said I had to. Ruby had her gallstones removed the day before and now she was at home sitting up in bed with this plastic pill bottle beside her on the table. I walked slow and scared to her. I walked with a little-boy walk and she propped herself up on the bed. I moved sideways with a slow step and then another slow step and then another. Then she took her plastic pill bottle and shook it in my face. It rattled like a rattle except it was full of something strange.

"What is it, Grandma?"

She shook them again and said, "They're my gallstones. All 21 of them. Doctor cut them out of me and let me take them home. He wouldn't let me take home the biggest though. He said he wanted to keep it on his desk."

Then she shook the pill bottle in my face *a rat a tat tat*. She said, "I'm going to make a flower bed with them."

Then she handed me the pill bottle and told me to put them in the flower bed. "Don't you eat them now, Todd."

I shook my head like she was crazy.

Then I went over to the window and opened the pill bottle and I put the gallstones in the bottom of a flower pot. "Nothing is growing," I told her. She told me they would. I didn't believe her.

The next day a flower was blooming.

And now…

A SECOND STORY ABOUT RUBY THAT WILL SHED LIGHT ON HER CHARACTER

I don't know who named AIDS cat AIDS cat, but Grandma always hated him. She always said, "You better stay away from them hogs," but AIDS cat never listened. He was AIDS cat. He had big patches of hair missing and he was all bony and skinny and looking like he was going to die any minute.

So one day we were outside feeding the hogs and she told AIDS to stay away from the hogs just like usual, but he wasn't listening.

Of course, AIDS cat used to go around and steal slop off the hogs. There was a knot hole in the slop bucket this big bad daddy hog used to eat out of. And so the big daddy hawg was standing at the trough eating the slop, and AIDS cat just kept sticking its head through the knot hole and eating some of that grub. AIDS cat did it once. And then he did it twice. Then he did it three times. He stuck his head through and scooped up some of the slop with a paw.

"You better watch it," Ruby warned him one last time.

He did it again and looked at us with a greedy grin.

So finally the big daddy hog had enough and reached up and bit AIDS cat's head plumb off—*gulp*. The cat's body fell back and jerked and jimmied and jerked some more, and the big daddy hog stood gobbling it on down. Ruby didn't say anything. She kept feeding the hogs and the pigs and then we went and sat on the front porch and watched the hummingbirds hum around. It felt peaceful.

So let us begin again then with the first chapter.

THE FIRST CHAPTER

I started to stay with Ruby and my Uncle Nathan when I was 14 years old.

It was around this time that Ruby ruined my birthday when she got breast cancer. I was in the kitchen when Ruby told me. She just looked at me and started shouting, "Oh lordie."

Then she started going on about how the doctor at Beckley said she had breast cancer and was going to die if she didn't have her breast removed.

My Uncle Stanley came to see us that evening, and I told him Grandma had cancer and was dying.

He just whispered "shit" beneath his breath and called the doctor up and it turned out she didn't have breast cancer at all but a benign growth that could *possibly* be cancerous.

The doctor said it could be treated with a cream.

She wanted everybody to think she had breast cancer though.

She started bothering the doctor so much over the next couple of months that he finally agreed to take her breast off as a preventative measure. She told him there was a history of it in our family. She was lying.

My Uncle Stanley started chewing her ass.

Ruby said: "Well all I know is I don't want to end up dying from it."

And Stanley said: "Ah hell, Mother, you don't have cancer from what I've heard. You just have a growth that at this moment is benign."

"Well he said he could take it off when I asked him. He said it's a preventative measure."

My Uncle Stanley said "shit" again. "Of course he said he could take it off. He's a damn surgeon. That's what he does. Surgeons are the worst people on earth. If you tell him to cut something off of your body, then he can sure as hell arrange it for you."

The day after the surgery was over we waited outside the room in the ICU.

The nurse brought out this jug of brown liquid they'd drained off of her, and then the nurse said we could go inside. So we all went in and gathered around Ruby's bed. She smiled and grinned with all of these IVs pouring out of her arm.

She pulled down her hospital gown and showed us how it looked all bandaged and stitched up and sunken. "It's not easy being a sick, old woman," she said.

My Uncle Stanley shook his head some more and whispered "shit" beneath his breath.

Then I looked at my grandma and she looked so lopsided to me. She looked so cut up and gone.

But then she pointed over to the old woman who was in the bed beside her. It was an old woman who wasn't saying anything but just staring up at the ceiling.

Ruby started telling us all about her. "That poor woman just cries and cries all night." Then Ruby said loud enough for the woman to hear it: "She doesn't know it yet, but before they brought her in I heard the nurses talking. They said the poor thing is full of tumors, and the family hasn't told her yet. They said she only has a couple more weeks to live."

My Aunt Mary said, "Shhhh," trying to tell Ruby to lower her voice. Then the old woman who just moments before looked dead, opened her eyes wide with a look on her face like: "What the fuck? What did you say? I'm dying?"

Of course, it shouldn't have surprised us when we came back to visiting hours later on that evening and Ruby was trying to sell a quilt. She was still bandaged up and sitting in the bed talking on the telephone to this woman on the 4th floor. "Now if you want this quilt you better call your daughter to bring you the money. Now I know you can't walk but you better find a way to get me the money. I'm in bed two."

But then some nurse came in and got all over her.

"Now Mrs. McClanahan, you get off that phone and quit trying to sell your quilts. You've just had a breast taken off and you need to rest."

Then the nurse took the phone from her and put it down.

"We don't allow people to come in here and solicit patients and we don't expect you to solicit your fellow patients to buy your quilts."

So the nurse left the room and Ruby started showing us the cards people had sent her.

She showed us a card from Mae and a card from Geneva that said, "Get Well Soon." There was a card from Leslie and Bernice and some flowers from Stirley and Brenda.

"I don't think anybody in here's got more pretty cards than I do," she said. "I know when Mae stopped by this morning she said she'd never seen so many cards and get well wishes. There was a woman from senior citizens who saw them. Said she'd seen more, but I know she's just jealous. She had a heart attack last year and didn't hardly get any."

Then she picked one up and held it in her hands. Since it just said "Ruby" on it she took a pencil from her nightstand and marked it out, because she could use this one over again for someone's birthday. She gave it to me and said happy birthday. I had just turned 14.

So it shouldn't have surprised us when we started hearing from other people about how it was a miracle Ruby survived cancer. One day Ruby came home after one of her senior citizen meetings. She had only been home for a few minutes.

She was sitting in her recliner, wearing a breast cancer survivor pin. She kept looking at it and saying: "I love my little pin."

Then she smiled and touched her pin again and said: "They threw a party for me down at the center and gave me this pin because I'm a survivor."

My Aunt Mary couldn't take it anymore.

She told Ruby she shouldn't be wearing a pin like that and telling people she had cancer. Mary told her the pin was for people who actually survived. It's not for someone who was just telling people she did. Then Mary said it's a wonder the surgeon didn't get sued.

So Ruby sat and thought about it for a while and said: "I know that's what one of the hateful women at senior citizens told me, but what does she know?"

Then she said her line: "Besides that, it was only a preventative surgery."

So Ruby sat for a long time and then she finally said: "Oh the poor things. It seems like you can't even go out of your house now without something horrible happening."

Then she thought about all the people she knew who were having bad things happen to them.

She talked about the little girl who had her foot run over by a riding lawnmower and lost her toes. She talked about how I came to live with her.

She talked about seeing her cousin, who was driving down the road and a rock slide crushed her to death.

Then she talked about her friend who just had her deformed leg amputated and couldn't get out of the house now.

And then she looked like if you just left the house something bad would happen to you, hurricanes, earthquakes, and then she grew quiet with another look on her face like something terrible was going to happen to all of us one day.

And you know what?

It will...

...if not tonight, then the next night.

THE NEXT NIGHT

The next night was radio preacher night. That only meant one thing. My Uncle Nathan was going to drink beer. I tried telling Nathan it was a bad idea to drink beer, but he wouldn't listen. My Uncle Nathan was 52 years old and still living with my grandma. He had cerebral palsy and couldn't talk. He just kept groaning and pointing at the beer and then pointing at his feeding tube. My hands were feeling kind of shaky as I popped open a can. "I don't know, Nathan. Grandma is going to get pissed again. She's just been home from the hospital for a few days and she's kind of edgy."

He just threw his hands up in the air and pointed towards the back room where she was doing her quilting and then he flapped his fingers like it was a mouth talking. That meant she was always running her mouth about something.

Then he pointed to the teddy bear sweatshirt he was wearing. He was still pissed that earlier in the day she had put the teddy bear sweatshirt on him. He groaned *goop oop* and had a look on his face that said, *Fuck her. I'm a grown ass man and she's making me wear a teddy bear sweatshirt.*

So I undid the dressing on the tube and pulled out the plastic tube.

"Are you sure?" I said and moved the beer to the tube.

He pointed to the tube and threw his hands up. That meant, *Get on with it.*

He tapped himself on the side of the head because he was smart. What was the use of drinking beer when you could immediately pour a six-pack in your stomach tube and have it shoot into your bloodstream that much quicker? I poured the beer in and then I poured another. Then I cracked another and another. Then I did the rest. He smiled and then he burped. It smelled like a beer burp. I cleaned up his tube and taped it back to his stomach and pulled down his teddy bear sweatshirt. Then he pointed to the radio. He wanted to turn it on.

"Ah shit, Nathan," I said. "I don't want to listen to the preacher tonight."

Nathan did though.

He waved his hands and started listening to the preacher going on about hell fire and damnation and the Day of Judgment awaiting us all.

Nathan shook his finger and told the preacher: *Tell them. That's right, tell them sons of bitches.*

Then he moved his little finger above his head which meant, *the good lord's coming to get us soon.*

I put the beer cans in a paper bag and hid them outside.

It was a good thing I did too, because just a few minutes later Ruby came into the room. She was still stitched and bandaged up but she was walking around at least. She said: "That's right Nathan—the good lord's coming to get you soon."

When Nathan wasn't telling preachers to give people hell, he was talking about his favorite, Benny Hinn. He pointed over to the counter where there was a Benny Hinn book.

He pointed up into the air.

I said: "What are you talking about?"

Ruby said: "Oh he's talking about this little girl the preacher healed the other night. Poor little girl was all crippled up and couldn't walk. The preacher prayed for her."

So Nathan nodded his head yes and pointed to his eye. That meant: *I saw it*.

Ruby said: "He was so excited about it he couldn't even sleep—poor little feller."

I told Nathan I didn't believe in preachers.

Nathan threw his hands up high again and groaned and pointed to his head like it was true.

I told him: "Ah hell, Nathan, these preachers are just ripping people off. You know what they say? 'I want to be a Baptist preacher/I want to join the Baptist church/I want to be a Baptist preacher because I don't like to work.'" I giggled and reached to the table and said: "I know you got your money hid for a reason."

I pushed back the table cloth where he always hid his money. It was still there—crisp five dollar bills.

So Nathan laughed and giggled because I knew where he kept his radio preacher money.

It was our secret.

The preacher kept hollering. I helped Grandma put away her dolls. Earlier that day, she was looking at them.

Grandma and I were going through her doll cabinet, and then all of the sudden Grandma went "shush."

I shushed and then she said: "Listen. Nathan sent the radio preacher five dollars this week. And the little feller's listening to hear if he says his name or not."

I giggled and listened to the radio preacher rattle off the names of all the sick and dying and the dead and the recently dead and the need to be dead.

Then he said all of these names so that people could remember them in their prayers.

Let's remember sister so and so in Beckley who just had surgery.
Let's remember sister so and so who has arthritis and wrote in recently requesting your prayers. Let's remember the church's hot dog sale this week. Let's remember sister so and so who's been having heart trouble since last week.

Grandma whispered: "I think he's going to say it."

We both listened.

We walked back towards the kitchen.

The preacher said: "And now I'd especially like for you to remember a special listener to this program."

Nathan listened.

We listened.

And then...

"I'd especially like for you to remember little Nathan McClanahan who lives with his mother in Danese, West Virginia. Now Nathan has cerebral palsy and he listens to this program every week. He loves the lord and so I'd like for you to remember him and his five dollar donation. His mother has just recently recovered from surgery."

Nathan burst out laughing.

He laughed and then he laughed some more.

He kicked and stomped his foot and threw his head all around.

Ruby patted his back and said: "That's right, Nathan—the preacher said your name on the radio. I told you he would. I told you—since you sent him that five dollars."

Nathan sat at the table and he didn't even moan or groan. He sat listening to the rest of the radio preacher with this mischievous look on his face. For a moment I thought to myself that I didn't know whether he believed or not. He believed in six-packs poured into feeding tubes. I didn't know whether he believed in heaven and faith and souls flying high into the sky and the good lord above, or if at the end of the day, all he wanted was to just hear his name on the radio.

Then I saw a look in his eyes like he was famous now.

He had a look in his eye like he was just days away from hanging out with movie stars and having sex with supermodels. He was famous now and he wouldn't ever wear teddy bear sweatshirts anymore. He was best friends with the most famous person in the whole fucking world. He was best friends with God.

So later that night, I rolled him into the living room. He sat and watched the preacher Bennie Hinn on the television. I sat down and watched it with him too. Bennie Hinn had his comb over and he was dressed in a white suit. He brought out this little girl with leg braces on. He asked her how old she was and she told him nine years old.

She was halfway crying, and so Benny Hinn crouched down on a knee and talked to her and he told her she was a beautiful little girl and that the lord loved her and Benny Hinn loved her.

He told her that the lord would come one day and get all of us and we wouldn't have to worry about these bodies.

So Nathan threw his hands up in the air like he always did, which meant *when I die just throw me in the backyard and let the raccoons have me.*

He laughed and watched Bennie Hinn start praying overtop of the little girl.

He threw his hands up again, saying *ahhhh. That's right, when I die just throw my body in the backyard.*

Out of the corner of my eye I saw Nathan sitting there.

His head was bowed and he was praying.

And then he was giggling.

He was still giggling later that night when Ruby put him to bed.

I thought, *My god, she treats him like a child. He's an old man, but she'd still breast feed him if she could.*

Then I went into the other room and read as Ruby tucked him in.

"Yeah that's right, Nathan, everybody's praying for the little girl," she said.

Nathan held his finger up above his head and wiggled it around because the good lord was coming for us soon and would take away these piece of shit bodies.

"That's right, Nathan," Ruby said. "The lord's coming soon. And he sent little Scott to look over us."

Then she tucked him in and kissed him goodnight and turned out the light until it was only the black ass country dark surrounding us.

Then he giggled a giggle like he knew something we didn't know.

He giggled a giggle because we were all a bunch of freaks.

He giggled a giggle because he knew we were the crippled ones.

Then he got a look on his face like he was thinking about something sad. It was like he was thinking about graveyards again.

GRAVEYARDS

I didn't even want to go to the graveyard, but Ruby told me I had to. She was giving my Uncle Stanley hell about it for weeks until he finally said: "Oh shit, Mother. That old road up there is rough as hell. What are we going to do if I get my truck stuck up?" My Uncle Stanley just lived down the road so he always had to take us places.

But she kept going on and on about it, saying: "Oh lordie, I'd like to go to the cemetery. I don't know when I'll get back up there."

She told us there was a grave up there she wanted to put flowers on.

There was a grave up there she needed to see before she died.

My Uncle Stanley finally gave in. He picked up some plastic flowers from the dollar store and drove her up to the graveyard in his truck. He drove down into Prince and we listened to the radio—99.5 The Big Dawg in country. *Lord have mercy, baby's got her blue jeans on.*

We drove through the places where Ruby had given birth to babies in shacks that no longer stood, and where my grandfather sold moonshine. We gunned it up Backus Mountain with my

Uncle Nathan, sitting in the back of the truck trying to hang on with his palsy legs. Then we finally pulled up the hill and into the Goddard graveyard.

Stanley stopped the truck and on top of the cow paddy hill we got out.

He said: "Damn it's bad enough being buried up here, let alone having to come up here when you're still alive."

But my grandma wouldn't listen to him and started walking through the grass. I remembered to watch my step because my Uncle Larry stepped in cow shit one time up here when he was wearing flip flops.

I told Ruby I didn't like graveyards. She told me it didn't matter.

Even though I was only 14 years old there was no telling when the angel of death might come to get my ass.

I stepped over a big fossilized cow paddy and then I stepped over another as Uncle Nathan laughed at us from the truck.

Earlier that day she fed me peanut butter fudge she made and told me nothing lasts.

Now we walked past the graves of all the people she knew.

There was Grandmommy Goddard and Daddy Goddard and Great Grandmommy Goddard and Virginia Goddard.

And there was her Aunt Mag Goddard who starved herself to death. Ruby stood in front of the grave and said, "No one knows why. She just locked herself in her room and starved herself to death."

Then there were other graves and she started walking through them.

She said: "I don't think they've been mowing it very nice out here."

Then she stopped in front of one.

I asked her if it was her mother.

And Grandma said, "Yeah that's Mommy. The day of the

funeral they tried putting her in the ground facing the west. I just hollered and carried on 'cause she was facing the wrong way for the resurrection."

Then she was quiet and smiled a gummy grin.

Then she walked on.

"Oh look at all the little graves," she said, walking past the grave of her uncle.

She turned to it and said, "They had to bury him on his stomach. He always said he never could sleep on his back. So he had them bury him on his stomach."

Then she said she never could sleep on her back either.

She had me pull away some tall grass from the graves.

She said that it seemed like all there was to do anymore was die. That's all people did in this day and age. She said she couldn't even get the ambulance to pick her up anymore when she needed them. Of course, I knew that they stopped coming because she called everyday claiming she was dying. When they got her into the ambulance, it seemed like she was always feeling better and just needed them to take her down to Roger's and get a gallon of milk. Finally one of the ambulance people told her: "Now Miss Ruby, you call us when you're having an emergency, not just when Nathan runs out of 7UP. The tax payers can't be paying for your trips to get Nathan's 7UP."

But I didn't say anything about it. She walked away from the graves and I noticed all the tiny plots beside her mother's grave. There was a grave here and then there was a grave there—the stones all broken off and covered up by the grass.

"Whose graves are these?" I asked and then I wondered. "Why all these little graves?"

I knew the answer. They were baby graves.

I walked away, looking at the end where Ruby was.

And I thought about her own mother losing baby after baby

after baby after baby after baby and still going on—surrounded by the graves of sons and daughters, brothers and sisters who never were. They were in this ground—all this great big lump of flesh we call earth.

I had even looked in the back of Ruby's mother's Bible with all of it written in the back. There was a date and then—baby died. There was a date and then—baby died. There was a date and then—girl baby died.

So I said, "You want me to put the flowers down here? Are these the graves you wanted to see?"

But Grandma just shook her head.

She pointed to a couple of graves at the edge of the mountain and said, "That's where I want to put them."

I thought, *THANK GOD.*

Ruby moved her walker and started moving closer to the graves, past the grave of her own little baby who died, and then past her husband, my grandfather Elgie who died of his fifth heart attack when I was three.

I heard my Uncle Stanley from far over at the edge of the field say: "Daddy would have shit himself if he knew you put him up here with all these goddamn Goddards."

Ruby got mean and said: "Well I figured I wanted him where I wanted him. And I put him where I put him."

She hobbled along some more and I walked behind her.
She said: "This is the grave I wanted to see. This is the grave."
I asked: "Whose grave is it?"

I walked in front of the stone and I saw it was her grave. It was the grave of Ruby Irene McClanahan, born 1917 died…

Then there was a blank space—the space where they would put the date of her death.

She touched the shiny stone and explained how Wallace and

Wallace gave her a really good deal on the tombstone. She told me I should start saving. It was a good investment.

So Grandma pointed to the grave and finally told me to put the flowers down. And that's just what I did. I put the flowers down on my grandmother's grave. Then she reached into her purse and pulled out a camera.

She said: "Well come on now, Todd. You want to have your pictures taken by Grandma's grave?" I told her for the thousandth time. "My name's not Todd, Grandma. My name's Scott."

My Uncle Stanley shouted at her: "Ah hell, Mother. Just leave him alone. He doesn't want to touch your grave."

Then she started in on my Uncle Nathan who was still sitting in the back of the truck. "Hey Nathan. You want to come and sit in front of Mother's grave? It's a pretty thing."

Nathan just sat in the back of the truck and shook his head like: *Fuck no.*

I finally gave in and Grandma took my picture next to her grave.

Then she waddled over to the side of the shiny marble tombstone and I took her picture.

I looked through the camera and all I could see was my Grandma Ruby standing beside her stone.

Ruby Irene McClanahan
Born 1917. And then the blank space.

Here was the date of her birth, and the date of her death, which we didn't know yet, but which we passed each year without knowing.

So I got ready to take the picture and I saw her smile.

I saw the graves filling up all around her and I saw how Grandma would be here beneath it one day and then Nathan and then one day Stanley, and then one day… me. So I saw her whisper, "Oh lordie," and claim she was dying like she always did.

I wished we were already back at home so I could eat some more peanut butter fudge. Nothing lasts.

I snapped the picture and it was like she was already gone.

It was like I saw that she was dying right then—real slow—and she knew the secret sound. It's a sound that all of us hear. It's a sound that sounds like this. *Tick. Tick. Tick.*

AND NOW A MOMENT TO ONCE AGAIN REMEMBER THE THEME OF THIS BOOK.

The theme of this book is a sound. It goes like this: *Tick, tick, tick, tick, tick, tick, tick.* It's the sound you're hearing now, and it's one of the saddest sounds in the world.

TICK, TICK, TICK, TICK, TICK

That's all I could hear from the big RC COLA clock a few weeks later. *Tick, tick, tick, tick, tick.* We sat in her kitchen and Ruby flipped to this picture of a guy who looked like he was sleeping. Then she grinned without her teeth in and showed me another picture of a guy who looked like he was sleeping too. She showed me another and then another. I thought, *Why are all these people sleeping?*

She ran her fingers over the picture and I realized… That guy is not sleeping.

THAT GUY'S DEAD.

So I looked closer at the man in the picture and I saw that his face was all sunken and his hands were folded across his chest. Beneath his hands there was a little pocket Bible. He was dead all right. Dead as hell. So Ruby started telling me the story about him.

She started telling me about how he was my grandpa Elgie's brother and how he was running around with some guy's wife in Beckley.

Then she told me about how one day he was with the wife when the husband came home.

I guess the husband knew something was going on, but before Elgie's brother could get his pants up—the husband picked up a block of firewood and beat Elgie's brother to death with it. Ruby said you should never take your pants completely off if you're engaging in infidelity just in case you need to make a quick getaway. I agreed. So Ruby took a picture of him at his funeral and then she turned to the back of the photo which had his death date on it—7/8/52.

Then she turned to another picture and it was yet another picture of a dead person. It was an old woman (her Aunt Mag) with one of those made-up funeral home faces. And what was funny about this one was that there was a man posing for the picture by the dead body. He was smiling.

"Who's that?" I asked.

"Oh I don't know," she said. "Just some guy I asked to pose by the pretty flowers."

So I sat in the kitchen not really knowing what to think.

Grandma looked through all of her pictures of the dead and then she said: "Of course some people don't think it's right. They don't think it's right taking pictures of the dead."

Then she flipped back through all of the other pictures and looked at the one of Elgie's dead brother.

She closed her picture book and smiled her smile.

That evening we went to the Wallace and Wallace funeral home to pay our respects for a woman she knew. It was another woman who was coming home one day and the mountain collapsed on her. I especially didn't want to be at the funeral when Ruby took out her camera later. I'd been going to wakes with her for years now, and I'd even been to wakes at people's houses, something called sitting up with the dead. I thought about how I watched people picking the body up and holding it and petting the dead hair and crying. I thought about how they carried it around and cried. I knew something was up that night, sitting around in front of the casket, and I knew what it was when my grandma leaned over and said: "Why don't you take a picture for Grandma?"

"WHAT?"

She pointed to the body and tried handing me a camera.

"Why don't you take a picture for Grandma?"

Oh GOD no.

I sat nervous and shook my head. But she wouldn't stop it.

She kept trying to hand me the camera and saying: "You go on."

I took ahold of it and stood there even though I didn't want to. I didn't want to take a picture of this dead body in front of everyone.

There were a couple of pretty girls in the corner and they had a look on their face like, "What's he doing? Is he getting ready to take a picture of a dead body?"

There were a couple of people standing around the body. They were hugging and holding and hugging and holding each other and crying. So I stood looking at it all and couldn't take the damn thing.

Grandma cussed "shit" beneath her breath and tried getting my cousin Tina to do it for her instead.

"You take that camera and take a picture for Grandma," she said...

Then she pointed to the camera

...and then at the body

...and then at Tina.

Tina didn't want to take the picture either, but finally she took the camera out of my hand and turned to the body.

"That's right," Ruby said. "Grandma's just a poor, old woman who can't get up. Go ahead and take it for your poor Grandma and make sure you don't cut off the pretty flowers behind the head. Someone spent so much on that arrangement."

So Tina held the camera and Ruby said: "That's right." Then Tina snapped the picture—SNAP—and everyone looked around at where the camera flash was coming from.

I figured this would be the end of it, but it wasn't. The next morning I walked the film down to Rite Aid when Ruby was working on one of her quilts. She was still stitching one of her squares on when I came back from Rite Aid and put the film back down on the table. I told her they wouldn't develop them. I told her what they said.

"What?" Ruby said after I told her what they said.

I repeated it: "They said they couldn't develop pictures of dead bodies anymore. They said it's the policy."

Ruby just looked so confused: "You mean they won't develop pictures of people you know anymore. Well how are you going to remember them? How's an old woman gonna remember all of 'em?"

I said: "It's probably because of privacy laws and stuff. I'm sure there are not too many people bringing in pictures of dead bodies anymore."

So Grandma Ruby kept working on her quilt with this funny look on her face.

Grandma said: "Well that doesn't make any sense. These aren't strangers. They're my blood."

I shrugged my shoulders and I sat with Ruby as she stitched another stitch and said, "Don't make any sense to me. I know I used to get them developed all the time." And then she was quiet for a second and then she started telling me a story that didn't have anything to do with anything…

…She told me about how she used to ride the horse down into Prince with her grandmother. "We used to go peddling," she said.

And they didn't have anything, and I guess they sold canned preserves or quilts.

Then she told me about how they were going down the side of the mountain towards Meadow Creek one time and they heard this sound of what sounded like a wild animal crying.

They rode and the sound grew closer. They realized it was a baby crying.

It was all bundled up and put beside the path so if somebody came by they'd find it.

So Ruby asked her own grandma if they could stop and take the baby home.

Her grandma just shook her head no because they could barely feed themselves, let alone another baby. They left the baby there and Ruby said the last thing she remembered was the sound of that baby crying from far away and the mule moving away so slow.

She started stitching another square.

She looked at the squares of her old scrap quilt.

She looked so sad thinking about how Rite Aid wouldn't develop her pictures of the dead.

And even now, years later, I wish I had pictures of all the faces I once knew. I wish I had pictures of Ruby and quilts, Nathan and teddy bear sweatshirts, groans and moans and radio preachers.

So Ruby and Nathan, let us pretend that we will always be like this. Let us pretend that we will never die.

Let us meet at this address a thousand years from now. Let us meet in Danese alive and not dead, alive and not dead, alive and not dead.

*

I sure as hell felt dead when the phone rang and they told Ruby that I had been skipping school for the past two weeks. They told me if I didn't come back the next day we would be in trouble. The next day I went to school and was at least happy to see my friend Little Bill. He was wearing a toboggan. I had been friends with Little Bill forever. It wasn't that big of a deal except we had retard math together and the retard math teacher Mrs. Powell only had three rules. No hats. I was just sitting down with Frog who was telling me about his brother getting crabs. "My mom told him not to be messing with that girl." Frog said it was really sad. He kept telling me how his brother came home one night and finally told his mom that he had crabs. She was drunk and told him to put Raid on it. He didn't know she was joking. Then Frog laughed. "And that's what he did too. Shit ate through the skin and he almost lost his testicle."

I shook my head and laughed and watched Little Bill sit down in front of me with his toboggan.

I whispered to him, "What are you doing? You're going to get killed wearing that hat." Then Frog shushed me.

I finally realized what wearing a toboggan meant. Little Bill came from a big family who all had different last names. Some days they came to school wearing toboggans—even the girls. I looked up at the retard math rules: #1 No gum. #2 No talking. #3 No hats. And Little Bill just sat quiet. At first Mrs. Powell didn't notice. She sat in front of the class doing paper work.

One of the girls, Bobbie Jo, raised her hand. There was

something wrong with Bobbie Jo. She was always holding crayons and pretending she was smoking cigarettes. Then she would eat the crayons. She always went around saying, "I got Terry's ring," pretending that she was married to this poor guy in our class. It was either that or, "I'm going to sit on Terry's face." Terry never said anything. One time I watched this guy named Jody spit on her. She wore glasses and the loogie smacked against the lens of her glasses. It slipped down the lens. She cried and cried. After that whenever she got the chance she started telling on people.

So Bobbie Jo raised her hand and said, "Mrs. Powell, isn't one of your rules that we can't wear hats inside?"

Mrs. Powell wasn't paying attention but then she finally said: "Yes—that's right. No hats."

Bobbie Jo kept going: "Well why is Lil Bill wearing a hat then?"

So it started.

Mrs. Powell looked up and Little Bill put his head down.

"Bill, take off your hat."

Little Bill kept sitting there like he didn't hear her. He kept his head down.

Mrs. Powell said it again. "Bill, take off your hat."

Little Bill said, "I can't."

Mrs. Powell walked over to him. "What did you say?"

Bill said, "I can't."

We were all feeling for him now.

Mrs. Powell walked over to him and said, "What did you say?"

Bill said, "I can't."

"What?" she said again. "Take off your hat."

"Please no," Little Bill said.

"Take it off."

"Please no."

"Take it off."

"Please no."

TAKE IT OFF!

And so he did. He took off his toboggan real slooooooooooooooooowwwwwwwww. That's when we saw it. His skull was bald and shiny and bright and so pale that you could see the veins running all over beneath the white skin.

"He has lice," Bobbie Jo said. "His mother makes him shave his head when he gets lice."

One of the other kids said, "You're bald, Lil Bill. Did your mother do that?"

Little Bill tried thinking something up quick. He knew we were in 9th grade now. He knew he was too old to have lice. The only thing he could come up with was the wrestler King Kong Bundy. King Kong Bundy was bald. Little Bill was bald. Little Bill said, "I'm trying to be like King Kong Bundy. I want to be a wrestler. I want to be like King Kong Bundy."

Then he was walking around us showing us his wrestling moves, showing us his muscles. He wanted to be like King Kong Bundy. Goddamnit. He kept saying it like it was true, like he didn't have lice, like the whole world was one big stupid lie that he believed in his heart.

I told him it was okay. I told him the same thing during history class the next period. I told him to keep his head down and just read his Crapalachia history book and it would be okay.

So we read about the accidents of history. We read about the James River and Kanawha Turnpike, which was a one-lane road that passed by our house. It was the way west. George Washington and the Virginians built it, but the New Yorkers built the Erie Canal. The Virginians found out that water travel is faster. The Virginians lost. Therefore, New York became New York. But imagine if we would have won. Imagine Crapalachia as the center of the world. Imagine skyscrapers rising from the mountains.

I read about how Governor Arch Moore kept 100,000 dollars in a refrigerator in his office because he loved cold, hard cash.

I read about how to stuff a ballot box. Have the party boss at the end of the road in a truck start with a blank sheet of paper that is the size of a paper ballot. Send the first guy in with the blank ballot stuffed in his pants. On the way out have him hide the real ballot in his pants and put the fake ballot inside the ballot box. Take the real ballot back to the party boss. The party boss fills it out and gives it to the next guy who goes in and slips the filled in ballot in the ballot box and brings out the blank ballot. This goes on all day. This goes on all day and then the men are paid in liquor. This is how you get them drunk and steal an election fair and square. This is democracy.

Then Frog raised his hand and told the teacher, "Do you know that Charles Manson grew up in West Virginia? His mother was a prostitute in Clarksburg."
The teacher told him to be quiet.
Everybody laughed.
Frog told us again that it was true.

Then we read about how you build civilization. They built the Hawk's Nest Tunnel by digging a big ass hole in the side of a mountain. They used a bunch of poor people to dig it. A poor person means either their skin was dark or their accents were thick. That's the best way to do anything—get a bunch of poor people to do it. So they cut and cut into the mountain but there was a problem. They didn't wet the dust from the cut limestone—so the men developed silicosis. The men started dying by the tens and then the twenties and then the hundreds and then—the thousands? Since they were poor the company just buried them. There was an investigation a few years later but no one cared. They were poor people. The official statistic was 476 but the truth is over 1,000 of the 3,000 men lost their lives in a few short days.

And then we read about the number of coal miners killed.

In 1931: 1,456
In 1932: 1,192
In 1933: 1,051
In 1934: 1,214
In 1935: 1,216
In 1936: 1,319
In 1937: 1,399
In 1938: 1,077

We read about the Farmington disaster and how the smoke rose from the mine and the miners' wives ran to the mine to see if their husbands were dead. The wives waited outside the mine for their husbands, but their husbands never came. The company didn't pay the miners for the half day they missed due to their death in the explosion.

In 1939: 1,062
In 1940: 1,361
In 1941: 1,226

In 1922 my grandmother's uncle was stuck inside the Layland mine for three weeks after an explosion. When they pulled out the bodies, some of the shoelaces were missing. Some of the miners weren't killed. Some of the miners were so hungry they ate their shoelaces. They died of starvation.

I read about how this proves something. It proves one thing. It proves that poor people are not smart, and only poor people are desperate enough to work in a hole and then thank god that they have a job working in a hole.

Then I read about what happens to bravery. William Marland was governor of the state of WV. He tried to put an excise tax on coal and the industry broke his ass down. He started drinking. He disappeared in the '60s. A reporter from the Chicago Tribune was riding in the back of a Chicago taxi cab. He looked up at the name of the taxi cab driver. He said, "Hey you have the name of the former governor of West Virginia."
The taxi cab driver said, "I know. That's me. I was the governor of the state of West Virginia."

He was an old man. He was a drunk. He tried to protect and help the people once. This is what happens to you. You wind up a drunk, driving a taxi cab in the city of Chicago.

We read and we learned and then we smiled the smile of killers. We had the smile of Charles Manson inside of us.

Later that day someone must have said something about Little Bill's bald head and lice. But Little Bill didn't say anything. Little Bill just walked over and smacked the guy upside the head. Then he started kicking him. He reared back with his leg and kicked. The dude on the ground didn't saying anything else. The other guys the dude was with circled around. Little Bill laughed at them. Mrs. Powell was going to walk over and say something, but Little Bill shook his fist at her. He said, "What? You want some of this." Then we knew. We knew Little Bill really was on his way to being King Kong Bundy.

We knew we wanted to get lice too—so we could shave our heads and kick the shit out of people who gave us hell.

CHECKERS

I was getting tired of playing checkers with Nathan. I even told him a couple of months earlier that I wasn't going to play anymore because he was always beating me. But here I was playing checkers again for some reason.

I jumped one checker and then waited. He made a move and then I made another move. He made a move and pointed to the toys in front of his chair. It was a ceramic hog with these giant testicles hanging down in the back. There was a rubber frog and a plastic puppy and a small stuffed alligator, but he kept pointing at the hog balls. Then he pointed at his chest. I finally said, "Gosh, Nathan, I'm trying to figure out where I'm going to move my checker. I wish you'd quit pointing at the hawg nuts. This is part of the reason I don't like playing."

Then Nathan turned the hawg towards Ruby so she could see.

He pointed to the giant testicles and then to himself.

Ruby whispered "shit" beneath her breath and then, "Nathan, you quit talking filthy like that. Can't believe you put that filthy stuff out there."

Nathan laughed and pointed at the ceramic hawg and then back to himself, which meant: *I got big hawg balls all right, Mother.*

I made my move and he laughed again and pointed to the newspaper. Then he pointed to his finger. He was saying, *I'm going to get me a woman out of the paper without a ring on her finger.*

Then he spread his arms wide. I said, "Nathan you can't place personal ads for a big fat woman. No woman would answer that."

Nathan laughed and spread his arms real wide. W*ell if I'm going to get me a woman I want the biggest goddamn woman I can find. I want one so goddamn big I can't even get my arms around her big ass.* Ruby whispered "shit" beneath her breath and then he jumped my checker. He pointed to the newspaper again and then acted like he was writing. He was telling me that he was going to have me write to one after he beat me. Then I jumped one of his checkers and then another and then another.

I was winning. For the first time I was winning. "Maybe it was a good thing I took a couple of months off."

I thought that it was because maybe he was bragging so much that he wasn't paying attention. I jumped another checker and I said, "King me." He kinged me. I started moving all over the checkerboard. He wasn't even watching really.

My grandma told Nathan, "Well you're going to talk so much no one is going to believe what you say. It's going to be just like Mary."

THE STORY OF AUNT MARY

I never should have been on the ride. I begged but my aunt talked me into it. She was always saying, "When I was a size 2."

And then a few minutes later she said again, "When I was a size 2." Then she would remind you later in the day. "Of course, I haven't always been so big. I used to be size…" I knew all of this was a lie but I still got on the ride with her. I got on the ride and I sat on the right side of her. This was a mistake. The ride started up and my Aunt Mary was pulled by the G-forces to the right. I felt my hip bones rubbing together. My Aunt Mary was not a size 2 anymore. So therefore, I should warn everyone: If you're ever at the West Virginia State Fair do not ride the Tunnel of Love with my Aunt Mary. I repeat. Do not ride the Tunnel of Love with my Aunt Mary.

Or

YOU WILL REGRET IT!

*

Nathan threw his hands up in the air and then he pointed to his head.

Ruby said: "I know. I know. You'll end up saying things no one believes. She almost crushed poor little Scott to death."

Then Nathan made his move. I jumped him. He made another move. I jumped him. He made another move. I jumped him. Ruby sat in the corner talking to herself, "That's how the world works. Just one thing after another and no plan about it at all. Then something happens and it don't mean nothing." Nathan made another move. I jumped him. He only had one checker left. He moved it around with his finger, but there was no place to go. He stopped moving it. Then I jumped him.

I won. I was just about to say, "I fucking won," but then I saw that he was pointing at the personal ads in the newspaper and he wanted me to write a letter for him. He wanted me to say he had his own set of wheels. "Whatever," I said. "I'm going to kick your ass again."

So then he was putting the checkers back on the board and we were playing again. He jumped one of my checkers. I made a move. He jumped another one of my checkers. I made a move and then he jumped me. I wanted to tell him that this was the reason I hated playing checkers with him. I made a move and he jumped me. Then I saw him smile.

I saw his smile and I knew that he had let me win earlier. I sat and watched him jump my checkers, just like always, one by one. He pointed to his head with his finger. That meant he was smart.

"That's right, little Nathan," Ruby said. "You're a smart feller. The world's not smart but you are."

Then I saw myself getting my ass kicked. He pointed to the newspaper and I saw myself writing a letter that started:

You mentioned in your ad that you are a full-figured woman and were looking for a man who appreciated a full-figured woman. Well I'm here to tell you that I like my women like I like my fried chicken—a little bit greasy and with plenty of fat around the edges.

I saw myself writing about how his balls were the size of hawg balls, and he was a tough motherfucker.

I saw him jump my checkers and I wouldn't tell them about the feeding tube and how it smelled when there was nothing on his stomach. I knew that I wouldn't write about how I was afraid of him when I was little. I thought he was a monster. I thought cerebral palsy was the name you gave to the monster in every family. I wouldn't write about how he used to knock himself out to make me laugh. I wouldn't write about how my uncles were babysitting me when I was small and they were wanting to get rid of me for a while so they could have sex with their girl-friends. They put me on the roof and I was too scared to jump off, but Nathan groaned and moaned until Grandma came to get me. I wouldn't write about how people stared at him when I pushed him down the road. They stared and shook their heads. I knew there would be no letters sent in return.

I knew I would never write about Nathan's light blue eyes— eyes as blue as Christmas tree lights.

I knew I would never write about his soft heart. The softest heart I have ever known.

I knew he believed in something that none of us ever do anymore. He believed in the nastiest word in the world. He believed in KINDNESS. Please tell me you remember kindness. Please tell me you remember kindness and joy, you cool motherfuckers.

*

So he started watching soap operas all the time. He thought soap operas could teach him something about women and love. Every day he went into the living room and leaned up against his little cushion and watched the women on the soap operas live their lives through story.

He watched the women on the soap operas start falling in love.

He watched the women on the soap operas hit their heads and get amnesia and run off and leave their families.

He watched the people getting in car chases and running out of burning buildings just before they exploded.

I used to sit and watch them too and wonder if he thought this is what the outside world was like—that each of us had an evil twin we didn't know about, an evil twin that was out there somewhere trying to take over our lives and kill us.

Then one day we went to Beckley for Grandma's foot doctor appointment. After the appointment, I pushed him through K-Mart and Nathan wanted to buy a copy of the movie *South Pacific*. I asked why in the hell he was wanting to buy a stupid musical. He kept pointing to the cover. Then he took his hands and put them to his chest like he was squeezing his breasts. There was a picture of a woman on the cover who was wearing this itty bitty bikini.

I told him: "Ah shit, Nathan. This is not going to be a tittie movie. This is going to be a stupid ass musical."

But the poor bastard didn't listen. When he got home and put it into the VCR, instead of a woman in her itty bitty bikini, taking it off, and showing him her stuff, it was just a bunch of women in a G-rated movie, singing songs, completely clothed, about washing men right out of their hair.

So *SHIT*! We went back to watching soap operas. We went back to watching the shows about women who were married and trapped by their psycho, maniac husbands.

He watched women having their children taken away by philandering husbands. The husbands made it look like the women went crazy and committed them to insane asylums.

But there was one woman in particular he was obsessed with. She was a woman who was the most beautiful woman on the show.

He even had a picture of her from *TV Guide* taped up on the paneling beside his bed in the hall.

I watched him during his nap and he used to stare at her for hours like she was the one he loved.

I sat at the table with him one day and he started pointing at the newspaper beneath his chair (Ruby always put newspapers down in case Nathan spilled something). He used to sit at the table and struggle to eat a spoonful of mashed up food, or drink from a bottle of 7UP. So now he struggled with the bottle and Ruby whispered: "Now Nathan don't you get choked."

So he drank and finally pointed again to the newspaper beneath his chair and giggled.

Then Ruby talked for him and told me what he was saying.

"Old Nathan says he wants to get him a woman out of the personal ads."

Nathan giggled.

I sat and laughed at him and said: "Oh god, Nathan. There's no sense in you looking for a woman. These women are all liberated today from what I hear."

Nathan laughed at me and wagged his finger around and around his head like we were all crazy.

"I know you don't want a crazy one."

Ruby said, "No, he's looking for a crazy one."

Then he held his arms out wide. He wanted a big fat crazy woman.

I said: "Yeah, Nathan, you're gonna have a hard time finding you a woman who's gonna feed you let alone give you a bath."

Ruby said: "He don't care, just as long as he gets him one without a ring on her finger."

I said: "Well, Nathan, I'm sorry to tell you but there's probably not too many out there looking for a 50-year-old man who still lives with his mother. They usually want a man who has his own place."

Nathan giggled and pointed to his bedroom with a look on his face like—*Oh I have a place of my own.*

I wrote to one of them in the personal ads. We waited for weeks. We waited another week.

She never wrote back.

The next month Medicare gave him what he wanted though. Medicare sent over a home health nurse to help three days out of the week. Nathan had a look in his eyes that said, *Thank god for fucking Medicare.*

Her name was…

RHONDA

The first day she was there Rhonda walked by the table and Nathan smacked her on the butt.

Rhonda stopped and said: "Nathan you better keep your hands to yourself or I'm gonna tell your momma on you."

And then Ruby laughed from her La-Z-Boy behind the table and said: "Yeah old Nathan, he likes the women."

Then he smiled and laughed and threw his head back, circling his long skinny finger around and around his noggin which meant: *You're crazy. You're crazy.*

Then he pointed to the big ceramic hog on the table with the giant balls.

"What?" Rhonda said.

"Nathan says his man parts are like that hog," I told her.

He tried smacking her on the butt again. So Rhonda twisted Nathan's ear and went to put in a load of laundry. Then she did the next chore Ruby had lined up for her.

Over the next couple of years she started doing all kinds of things.

She cooked the dinner.

She washed the dishes.

She cleaned off all of Ruby's knick knacks.

She made the beds.

She ran the sweeper.

She moved the knick knacks so Ruby could see 'em better.

She ran the sweeper.

She picked up the medicine over in Rainelle.

She stopped at Rogers' grocery for Nathan's bananas.

She came back and cooked supper.

She washed the dishes.

She cleaned the bathroom.

She pushed Nathan in front of the television.

She put him to bed.

She listened to me tell her how I wanted to go away. I wanted to go away to school. I wanted to be a famous writer.

But Rhonda was really there because of Nathan's feeding tube. It was just a peg tube sticking out of his stomach and it was all pusy and nasty and sick-looking. It stunk too because you could smell the inside of his stomach. One time I was watching her feed him. He pointed down at the tube and complained about how it was stinking. Rhonda sat there getting ready to pour Nathan's Ensure into the feeding tube.

She was feeding him strawberry bubblegum Ensure and so she held the feeding tube and joked with him. "Boy, Nathan, this Ensure doesn't smell too bad."

Then she opened the Ensure and took a swig.

Nathan laughed and wiggled his finger around and around his head, before pointing at her: *You're crazy. You're crazy.*

Then he pointed at his feeding tube and held up six fingers which meant he wanted a six-pack.

Rhonda laughed: "Oh gosh, Nathan—I'm not going to get you a six-pack. You're about as bad as that man of mine."

Then Rhonda started talking to him. She poured the Ensure

in the tube and the tube sucked it down. The old tube *gurgled gurgled* and *gargled* and *gurgled* it all down.

After they were done Nathan touched Rhonda's leg and then he held Rhonda's hand and listened to her talk.

"Yeah, Nathan, Sean's been real mean here recently, drinking and hitting me."

Nathan took his hand and threw it towards the door and this meant: *Well kick his ass out.*

He pointed to his foot which meant, *I'll kick his ass for you.*

Rhonda smiled and said, "I know but where would I go?"

Nathan pointed to his bedroom.

Rhonda grinned and whispered, leaning forward: "And I could come in here and live with you? Is that what you're saying?"

Nathan nodded his head.

I didn't even think anything about it until a couple of months later when my Aunt Bernice came over and she was smoking her cigarettes.

She said: "Well I just hope everything works out all right."

I was like, "What? What are you talking about?"

Aunt Bernice smoked her cigarette and then blew the cigarette smoke *foooooo.*

Then she said: "Well I think it is obvious. He's in love with her. You can see it in his eyes. He's in love with her."

So I started paying closer attention. I realized it a couple of weeks later. I was sitting in the living room with Nathan, watching *Walker, Texas Ranger* and then Benny Hinn. Then Rhonda came in and said: "Okay, Nathan. It's time to go to bed."

Nathan shook his head and pointed to the clock for more time.

Rhonda said: "Oh no, you're the one who said you needed to be on a schedule. So we're gonna put you on a schedule. It's 9:30 and you know what that means?"

She stood him up and took off his sweatpants.

Then Rhonda put Nathan in the bed and started to tuck him in. Nathan just lay there and giggled and then he reached out and tried to touch her breasts. Now instead of moving like she usually did, Rhonda just sat there. Nathan reached out some more and touched her breasts again.

She said: "Nathan, you better not do that."

Then she was quiet and grinned: "You're rotten to your core."

Nathan touched and then touched some more. They weren't giggling anymore.

I went into the other room to leave them alone, but when I sat down on the couch, I could still see them saying goodnight.

Nathan sat up in his bed and Rhonda started doing the hand signals she used to help communicate with him. But now they were whispering to each other and I heard Rhonda say: "Okay now. I gotta go."

And then she pointed to her eye.

Then she pointed to her heart.

Then she pointed to Nathan.

Then Nathan was quiet and he did the same thing.

He pointed to his eye.
I.

Then he pointed to his heart.
Love.

SCOTT McClanahan / 49

Then he pointed to Rhonda.

You.

Rhonda kissed him goodbye and said: "Well you just look at my picture, and I'll be back in the morning."

And so she left and Nathan just sat there and looked at Rhonda's picture in the moonlight.

I tried talking to Nathan, but he was too busy looking at it.

And so he stared at the picture beside his bed.

It was a picture of Rhonda.

It was a picture of the woman he loved.

This went on until Ruby started getting jealous.

"He don't need no woman. All he needs is me," I heard Ruby say one day.

And then one evening Ruby told Rhonda right to her face: "Well you're just a fat old thing. Big around as can be."

Rhonda told Ruby she didn't have any room to talk. But then Rhonda started crying. She left. This went on for months.

After that Ruby started complaining about how Rhonda kept coming in late and how one night Rhonda didn't show up at all. Then one night Ruby told her not to come. Rhonda left crying again, and Nathan lay in the bed and didn't say anything. PISSED OFF.

The next day I went into Nathan's bedroom and he was still in bed.

I said: "How are you doing, Nathan?"

He didn't say anything.

I asked him how he was doing again.

He still didn't say anything.

I twisted his ear.

He didn't even act like I was there.

He turned over in his bed, staring at Rhonda's picture.

He started watching soap operas again, but then it happened. One day on the soap opera, the actress he loved was walking across the street, and her husband's crazy ex-wife hit the gas and ran her over. Her husband was there and held her in his arms as she died.

And so I imagine that Nathan just sat there unable to do anything, listening to her whisper, "I love you. I'm so sorry I didn't do more to love you. I'm so sorry. I'm so sorry."

And then… "I'll love you forever."

So Nathan watched her die and whispered it inside his head, *I love you too.*

And now it wasn't an actress anymore he watched on TV, but a beautiful woman he had loved for a long time.

WHAT HAPPENED?

So nobody really knows what happened. I was outside when I heard Ruby scream.

I came running inside. There was a drawer on the floor and newspapers. Ruby said, "I was in the back room and when I came back the poor thing was like this."

There was a set of knives on the counter beside the sink. He was in front of his chair. The chair was turned over. His legs were beneath the table. He was on his back. There was a steak knife sticking straight out of his chest.

There was an ambulance. Lights were flashing around and around.

There was a stretcher... ambulance guys... bringing Nathan out on a stretcher.

And then the back of the ambulance.

He tried to take his own life, but he survived. He didn't die.

So after Nathan's knife wound, he didn't do much of anything but sit around at the kitchen table and watch it all go by.

One day I was sitting at the table with him, and he leaned over on his elbow and started rolling his 7UP bottle back and forth like he was bored.

Back and forth.

Back and forth.

He breathed a soft sigh and batted his eyelids.

He had movie star blue eyes.

So he sat and I wondered if he was thinking about the fact that he was the one who stayed. He was the one who sat watching his younger brothers when they were little boys, and then watching them leave the house when they were grown men.

He was the one who stayed because he had to stay. He was the one who was sitting at the table now, where he was always sitting, remembering how his brothers returned with their young wives, all pink and pretty, and pretty and pink, and pink and pretty, and pretty and pink and pink and pink and with accents from faraway places.

And then a few years later, returning once more with pink children of their own.

So I felt his muscle and laughed, trying to make the quiet go away.

But he was quiet now because he knew he would never have

any of this. I saw what he saw sitting there—that there would be no brides or babies. There would be none of this. He blinked and breathed another soft sigh with a look on his face like...

Oh shit I'm trapped in my body...

Oh shit I'm trapped in my body.

And so there was no more Rhonda.

There was no more Rhonda until after Nathan died.

After the wake was over, and the funeral was over too, and everybody was walking away, I went back to pick up something, or help my aunt walk back through the mud.

I looked up, and when I did, all the way in the back of the crowd of people was a woman.

It was a woman all by herself.

It was Rhonda.

She was crying so hard that I thought she was going to fall down.

She was crying and her chest was going up and down, up and down, and she was trying to walk back to her car.

A couple of months later, on a bright evening, just before the sunset, I went by the grave. It was fall and there was this glow over everything, and it was so bright. And it was all still there—the gravestone and the old tree, and the old flowers were there too. But now there was something new in front of Nathan's gravestone. It was a little teddy bear covered in fur and there was a little note beside it. So I opened it up and saw a picture of a heart, and beneath the heart was a note that said, "I love you, and I'll always love you Nathan." It was just like in the soap opera. And then beside the heart was a single name. It said...

...Rhonda.

But wait.

I have decided to stop for a moment.

I want to stop for a moment before they die. I am not ready yet.

I want to stop and remember them for a moment as they were, when we were all together, when they were still alive. I want to remember Ruby's food and Ruby's table and Nathan's laugh.

*

On Sunday I sat and smelled the chicken and gravy, bubbling up all brown and beautiful. I stood and dusted all the JFK commemorative pop bottles—and spoons from the 50 states—and a bird clock chirp-chirping the time. It was a bird clock that chirped a cardinal at two o'clock and then an Eastern Woodlands Oriole at four o'clock. So if you were outside and heard a robin chirp you were fucked up the whole day thinking it was three o'clock.

Then I dusted the plastic frogs going *ribbet ribbet* every time I walked by.
I dusted the pictures of Jesus and footprints in the sand.
I dusted a bowl of bread glazed stiff for decoration and a shotgun sitting up behind the door.
I walked around the recliner and the radio playing radio preachers and gospel tapes.
So Ruby stood at the stove and I asked: "Grandma, where'd you get these flowers?"
My grandma said: "Oh Larry sent 'em to me. He sent me some to give to Mae too but I liked her flowers better so I just kept them both."
She was always doing stuff like this.

A STORY ABOUT RUBY TAKING STUFF

One day we went over to Aunt Shirley's and Shirley had just put this new mirror on the wall. Grandma said it was pretty. Ruby walked over and took it off the wall because she wanted it for herself.

Shirley said: "Ruby, you can't take that with you. That's mine."

Ruby said: "Oh but you have so much stuff." Then she put it under her arm and we left. Aunt Shirley just stood there.

*

I looked at Ruby now and I saw all of the things she knew.

She knew how to do all kinds of things no one else knew how to do.

She knew how to render lard and make soap.

She knew how to make biscuits from scratch and slaughter a hawg if she had to. And she knew how to do things that are all forgotten now—things that people from Ohio buy because it says homemade on the tag. I looked at the quilt she was working on. The quilt wasn't a fucking symbol of anything. It was something she made to keep her children warm. Remember that. Fuck symbols.

Then she said: "Okay, I think it's ready."

…We all sat down and started eating the chicken and gravy and I did it like this. I took a giant spoon and started scooping out all kinds of gravy all over my plate and plopped out a spoonful of mashed potatoes. Then I grabbed myself a chicken leg and got to it. I sat and first started eating all the gravy with a spoon. Then I looked out across the table, and there were cucumbers in vinegar, and homemade biscuits, mayonnaise salad, green beans, pickles, fried chicken, chocolate cake, angel food cake, chicken, brown beans, peas in butter, chicken, more biscuits, and gravy, gravy, gravy. Then Grandma started telling us about how my father was born on the kitchen table and how the doctor was drunk.

Ruby told us about how the doctor was really a dentist but would deliver babies. She told us how she gave birth to him on the kitchen table. After he was born he was so pretty and shining and new. She just held him in her arms—the prettiest baby you've ever saw, the prettiest baby she had. He was so pretty that the doctor offered to give her twenty dollars for him or trade him for another baby he had out in his truck. But she didn't trade him. She just held him close to her heart and listened to him whimper. We listened to the story and ate our chicken and gravy. Then I skimmed the bowl and got out a couple of more bites and it was all gone.

So after dinner was over I watched Grandma gather up all the dishes and put them in the sink.

Then Grandma said: "Well, Todd, you sure didn't eat much. You're just a skinny thing—look sickly."

But I didn't say anything about Todd not being my name.

She wouldn't listen anyway because she was on to something else now.

I started washing the dishes and then she started going on about how I didn't need to throw away the styrofoam plates because she could use them again.

I said: "Well you can't wash styrofoam plates and use them again. It's not healthy. You can't get them clean."

But Ruby just told me to wash them and said: "Well that's all right. That's the reason I got something."

After dinner I took a nap and I dreamed a dream about the future and in this future I was dreaming a dream about the past. But in my dreams I'm always back at Ruby's house, and back at Ruby's table. It's always Sunday again and we're all just sitting around the table like we always did. Nathan's on one side and I'm on the other and my grandma's on the left. And just like always she's fixed chicken and gravy and we're all so hungry and passing the plates—the biscuits, the mayonnaise salad, the cucumbers in vinegar, and I think to myself, even now, that this will be what the final moments of oxygen escaping from my brain will be like. It'll be like a Sunday so long ago with all of the dead stuffing themselves full of food cooked with lard, and gravy that will once again clog their arteries and kill their hearts. It will be the feast of death and it will taste so delicious.

Then I dreamed that she was gone and yet, even now there's still something about me that believes I can bring her back from the dead. There's something in me that wants them to rise from the grave and go back there. There's something about me that wishes I could see them again.

But wait! There's still something that makes sense.

There's still the recipe for chicken and gravy. There may still be something of Ruby inside of it. So here's the recipe…

Ingredients
1 (3 pound) frying chicken, cut up
2 cups of buttermilk
1 teaspoon of garlic powder
1 teaspoon of onion powder
1 teaspoon poultry seasoning
Vegetable oil for deep frying
Butter
Flour

Directions

Wash chicken and pat dry. In a large bowl, stir together buttermilk, garlic powder, onion powder, flour and butter. Place chicken in buttermilk mixture and refrigerate.

In a large cast iron frying pan, heat oil to 325 degrees F. Drain chicken in a colander to remove excess buttermilk. Place flour and butter in a large paper bag. Add chicken. Close top and gently shake bag to coat chicken with batter mix. Remove chicken and fry, turning pieces over after 3 minutes. Continue to fry, turning until brown on all sides.

And if you're reading this—you can go into your kitchen and try making it right now. And even if you don't know how to cook, wherever you are, and far away into the future, maybe you can make this chicken and gravy and we can bring these zombies back to life again.

YOU CAN'T PUT YOUR ARMS AROUND A RECIPE

I had to take Nathan to the bathroom. It had already been a horrible day. That morning on the way over to the doctor's office my grandma kept going on about Nathan grabbing the steering wheel and killing us all. I had just got my license and Nathan was sitting in the passenger seat. Ruby was full of anxiety in the back and then she said it again, "Now, Nathan, don't you grab the steering wheel and wreck and make us crash over the mountain and kill us all." Nathan just shook his head like *Fuck. Do you seriously think I'm going to grab the wheel and wreck us? Do you really think that?*

Then he circled his finger around and around his head and told her she was crazy.

I said, "He's not psychotic, Grandma. He just needs a wheelchair."

Then we had to wait a couple of hours before the foot doctor could cut Grandma's toenails. Now here we were eating at Captain D's and Nathan had this look on his face. That look meant one thing: He had to go to the bathroom. He had to go to the bathroom BAD.

So I got up from the booth and took hold of his wheelchair

when Ruby stopped us. She reached into her giant purse and pulled out his pee bottle inside a plastic bag. Then she handed it to me. I just laughed and said: "Well, Grandma, you don't have to show off the pee bottle to everyone." Nathan just waved his finger and stomped his foot which meant: *I don't even need the pee bottle. I need to go the other thing.*

Ruby told us we might need it. You never know. Then I put the pee bottle on Nathan's lap and started pushing his wheelchair to the bathroom when she thought of something else. "Little Nathan, you need these too." Then she pulled out a fresh pair of boxer shorts she kept in her purse. Nathan lowered his head.

I took the pair of boxers and put them in my back pocket. I tried to make a joke about it to make it less uncomfortable. "Shit, Nathan, you're like a superhero. I need to start carrying around my own change of underwear."

Nathan didn't say anything and just held the pee bottle on his lap. We passed the other people who were sitting in their booths. They looked up from their greasy fish and watched us pass. They were staring at Nathan and his pee bottle. Nathan stared back and held his pee bottle. I tried making another joke, "Hey, Nathan. You ever drink beer out of that pee bottle before? If we get lost on the way back home we can use it as a canteen."

But he didn't laugh.

He needed to go to the bathroom.

So I stopped in front of the men's bathroom and tried to open the door, but it was locked. *SHIT.* I told Nathan that someone must be inside. Nathan tapped his foot against the ground. He needed to go to the bathroom. I couldn't stop talking, "You know it probably looks funny two guys going to the bathroom together. This is the kind of place where two guys going to the bathroom together could get their asses kicked."

Nathan didn't laugh. He tapped his foot and we waited. Then a Captain D's employee said something. So I walked over to her and left Nathan in front of the door. She said, "That bathroom is out of order. You're going to have to use the ladies' room."

I nodded my head and walked back to Nathan who had a new look on his face. It was a look that said, *I need to use the bathroom. I need to use the bathroom. I need to use the bathroom.*

I told Nathan we were going to have to use the ladies' room. I started to move him towards the bathroom, but then I saw an old woman out of the corner of my eye. "Mam," I said, but it was too late. She was already inside.

The door lock popped.

Pop.

Nathan lowered his head.

SHIT. SHIT. SHIT. SHIT. SHIT. SHIT.

"It's okay," I said. "Just hold it a little while longer. Just a little while longer."

I bent over and whispered into his ear. "It's going to be even weirder now. Two guys going to the ladies' room together."

I rested my foot against the back of the wheelchair and we waited. "Just a little while longer," I said.

We waited.

We waited.

The toilet flushed. The old woman came out.

"Oh I'm sorry," the old woman said.

I smiled and nodded my head. Then I smelled. It was too late.

So I kept the door open with my foot and pushed him inside. I took the boxer shorts out of my back pocket and put them on the sink. Then I took off his Velcro tennis shoes and put them in the corner. I took his white tube socks off and put them in his Velcro tennis shoes. I looked at the bathroom wall. It had a box that said: "Sanitary napkin disposal bags."

"Do you have any tampons or maxi pads that you need to throw away." Nathan still wasn't laughing. He wasn't laughing at anything now.

I took his sweatpants off and looked at them. "It's okay, Nathan. There's nothing on them. We're okay."

Then I folded them and put them on the side of the sink too. I took out about thirty paper towels and I put about half of them beneath the faucet and made them wet. Then I turned to Nathan. He was looking away.

I said, "Do you think if I stand you up—you can lean against my shoulder?" Nathan moved his hand which meant yes. I took hold of his arms and picked him up. He leaned against my shoulder. A piece of crap fell out of the leg of his shorts and hit the ground. Nathan groaned. "It's okay," I said. I took one of the wet towels and picked it up and dropped it in the toilet. Then I took his boxer shorts and slid them down.

"Okay, lift your leg," I said. I slipped them off.

He groaned.

I was sweating now.

Then he lifted his other foot and I slipped them off and threw the underwear away.

I felt Nathan getting wobbly, so I stood up.

He grunted *ughhh*. I threw my arms around him and held him up. He was breathing heavy. I was trying to keep him up, but he went down on his knees and then on his side. "Okay. Okay," I said and tried to help him down. "I know it's hard for you to stand like that."

Ughhh, he grunted and pointed at the paper towels.

"I'm going as fast as I can," I whispered. I took the white towels and I wiped him. Then I threw them in the trash. Then

I took the dry towels and wiped him some more. I picked up his fresh pair of boxer shorts and put them on him. They were all bunched under his hip because of the cold floor. Then I took his sweatpants and socks and shoes and put them on too. I helped him sit back up. Then I turned to lift him. My arms were too tired.

Ughh, Nathan said.

I stood up and tried to catch my breath. "Okay, just give me a second." Then I put my arms underneath his armpits and heaved him up into the wheelchair.

In the end I just stood there and caught my breath. I threw away the rest of the paper towels. I patted Nathan on the back, but his head bowed.

"You ready?"

I twisted his nose like I always did, but he didn't smile.

He took his finger and pointed it to himself and then pointed it to me.

"What did you say?"

So he took his finger again and pointed it at himself and pulled the trigger.

I knew what he was saying.

"You're wanting me to shoot you?" I said.

He nodded his head yes.

He was wanting me to shoot him.

I giggled but then I stopped.

He wasn't joking.

So I pushed him out of the bathroom.

His eyes were saying, *You should be staring at me. I'm beautiful.*

His eyes were saying—*Life is not short. Life is way way way way way way way way way too long.*

SO

I was over at Little Bill's when the phone rang. It was my Uncle Stanley. He said they had to rush Nathan to the emergency room.

I borrowed Little Bill's car and I drove all the way back through the dark mountains until I came to the interstate, and then I turned my high beams on and sped towards the hospital, thinking to myself, *Please don't let him die yet.*

I flipped my high beams off because there was a tractor trailer passing in the other lane.

He passed, so I flipped them back on again and whispered, "Please don't let him die until I get there."

I wanted to see him die.

But he wasn't dead yet. He was on the 3rd floor of Appalachian Regional Hospital and my Uncle Stanley was standing in the corner of his room. So I walked over to his bed and stood beside Stanley. Nathan was just there in the bed. His eyes were closed. There were tubes coming out of his nose and tubes coming out of his mouth. There was a shit smell in the room because the nurse had just changed his pants from where he shit himself. His breath was heavy. Every time he breathed—*huh*—it sounded like somebody was knocking the wind out of him—*huh*—every time he breathed.

It scared me—*huh*—the way he breathed like that. *HUH.* So I just stood and listened to Nathan breathe his booming breaths—*huh*. I thought that everything I thought about death was wrong.

I shook my head and followed Stanley into the waiting room where we sat and waited for something to happen.

And then we went back and forth, back and forth. At the end of the hallway there was a crazy old woman who didn't even know where she was at and she kept shouting, "Louise. Louise."

The nurse came over and said, "There's no Louise here, honey."

Then the nurse said: "Why don't you help fold these quilts for your babies."

The old woman picked up these hospital towels and started folding them.

The nurse said: "Yeah, you're doing a good job folding these quilts for your babies."

I thought, *This world is crazy.*

We walked around for another three or four hours going back and forth to Nathan's room every fifteen minutes or so.

And then the last time I went into his room before we left, Aunt Mary was leaning overtop him crying and telling him, "You just fight, Nathan. You just fight."

She left.

I stood at the foot of the bed and told him inside my head, *No, Nathan. You go ahead and die.*

Nathan just kept breathing his booming breaths, *HUH HUH.*

Then Stanley said: "Well we might as well go." So about 4:00

that morning we left the hospital and drove all the way back to Danese.

I drove behind my uncle's truck and saw a dead deer on the side of the road. At the bottom of Sandstone Mountain I saw an old guy walking through the darkness with a backpack. He turned towards me and lowered his thumb and it looked like Nathan, traveling somewhere. I shook my head and drove all the way back home trying to stay awake. When we finally got home we hadn't so much walked through the door and the phone rang.

My uncle picked it up and said, "He did. Okay. Thank you."

Then he hung up and his voice was all choked up and full of tears. "That was the hospital. He died. I'll have to tell mother."

I went "Oh" and my Uncle Stanley walked outside.

So that morning I started planning for Nathan's wake. I asked Ruby what she wanted him buried in. She told me she wanted him buried in sweatpants and a sweatshirt just like he always wore.

She said, "He never liked those suits and ties—awful things."

So I went over to Wal-Mart and bought him a white sweatshirt and a pair of white sweatpants.

And then I took them up to the cashier who said, "Did you find everything?" thinking I was just a guy buying a sweatshirt and sweatpants.

She didn't know I was a guy who was shopping for clothes to bury his uncle. That afternoon when I took the clothes down to Bob Wallace, I said, "I need to get him a t-shirt too so that he won't get cold." The funeral home guy just looked at me.

Then I laughed because he was just a dead body now and it didn't matter if he was cold or not.

So all of the children and all of the grandchildren and all of the great grandchildren and all of the mothers and all of the uncles' uncles and all the cousins and all of the cousins' cousins—they all came in and we had a wake. That night we walked into the wake where the casket was.

And then I walked up to the coffin too and looked down at Nathan. I whispered, "What are you now?"

The coffin was so full of stuffed animals that my Uncle Stanley said: "Need to tell people to quit putting stuffed animals in there. It's gonna be so full of stuffed animals they're not gonna be able to see the body."

I giggled and looked at Nathan. I looked at his plastic-looking skin, and I looked at his lipstick red lips, and I looked at his cheeks painted rouge red.

"They've turned you into a cross dresser, Nathan. They put lipstick on you."

I thought, *You're the deadest-looking body I've ever seen.*

So everybody passed the body and said goodbye. Ruby balanced herself on her wheelchair and stooped to kiss his face. There were people in the corner sharing recipes and there were people telling jokes. There were people crying in the corner. There were people saying that God has a plan for all of us. I said, "People are meant to have cancer or find out that their child is a serial killer? That's a pretty shitty plan."

People gave me dirty looks.

There was this little girl who was taking violin lessons. She stood up and was going to play us a song.

One of the old women said: "Oh look at that little girl. She's so cute. And she's gonna play us a pretty little song."

So the little girl took out her bow and her violin and everybody listened as she drew back her bow across the strings—*eek—squeak.* Then she brought it back *eeek—squeak.* And she was playing the worst sound you've ever heard. It made your stomach hurt, it sounded so bad. It made you want to die.

Then just a few minutes before the wake was supposed to end, my Uncle Terry came in. He'd flown in all the way from San Francisco. His wife was pregnant and she was getting ready to have a baby. He was upset because he wanted Nathan to be able to hold his first child. So he came in at the end of the wake holding something in his hands. He walked up to the coffin and put something in Nathan's hand. Then he patted the dead hand and walked away. It was an ultrasound picture of his baby who wouldn't be born for another four months. But Nathan was holding his baby now. Nathan was buried with a baby in his hands.

The next day at the funeral they put Nathan into the ground. It was cold and rainy and the ambulance brought Ruby out on a stretcher. She was all covered in quilts and her head was wrapped in blankets so she wouldn't get cold. She was back away from the coffin, propped up on the stretcher, and the preacher stood at the grave shouting loud so she could hear. I stood, watching and listening to it all. Before long I wasn't listening to him anymore. I was looking out over the graves and watching my cousin Bonnie walking with her little boy Paul and showing him all the graves. This was his great grandmother. This was Paul's great grandfather. This was the one thing we shared with everyone. This was the story of generations and they begat and begat and begat. Death.

And so the preacher prayed and preached and prayed some more. Then after the preaching was done Wallace and Wallace brought over this white box full of doves and the preacher said: "We'll now release this white dove which is a symbol of the dearly departed's soul."
The preacher pulled off the top of the box and the white dove shot out and over all of us and then high up into the cold

gray sky and then even over the old home place, where it circled twice before flying away.

Then Preacher Steve raised his arms and shouted: "He's flying home to heaven, Ruby. His soul is flying home to heaven."

Ruby said: "Oh lordie, yes. Little Nathan is flying home to heaven."

Preacher Steve shouted: "Hallelujah, Ruby."

Ruby raised her arms too and shouted "Hallelujah" as the white dove disappeared into the sky.

And then everybody started walking back towards the trucks to go home. I looked in front and saw the little girl from the night before with her evil violin. She was putting her violin beneath her chin and getting ready to play us one of her monster songs. So we rolled our eyes and shrugged our shoulders like, *Oh god, not again.*

I imagined myself choking the little girl to death, beating her to death with her violin.

Then Stanley bent over and put a five dollar bill into her case like he was hoping that would stop her. But it didn't. She just took her bow and started moving it across the strings until it squeaked—*eeek*. And then *eeked squeak*. And then squeaked *eeek*. And we covered our ears. But then she slowly moved the bow once more and suddenly she wasn't the horrible little girl playing her horrible violin, but the greatest musician you've ever heard, playing the most beautiful song in the world.

Then I shut the book and looked at the dark mountains. It wasn't my blood or face or nerves. It was dirt and rocks and the smells of skin. I looked out into the purple mountaintops and laughed because I stood on these mountaintops, but then I felt the meanness. I felt myself hating because I had been in the darkness of what was between the mountains. I saw the crazy ass god of the old book people who made his story. They made him the way they made him because they lived next to a crazy river. I saw the people of the desert smile because of the Nile. Then I saw these mountains and chunks of mountains smile and I knew one thing.

I felt darkness because I had been deep in the hollers, and I knew glory because I had stood on top of the beautiful mountaintops. More mountaintops please. More mountaintops.

This is a lie I was told as a child, but it's still true. The New River is one of the only two rivers that flows directly north. The other one is a river called the Nile. Those rivers are inside of me. I have a river inside my heart. You have a river inside your heart. There are diamonds inside of both of us. We are all flowing north.

I understand that Nathan was gone now. And I knew that this was a different part of my life now. This is where the hero goes out into the world and encounters the people he meets along the way. This is the part that comes after the first part. This is a part called…

THE SECOND PART

So time passed. After Nathan died, Grandma went to live with my Uncle Stanley and I needed a place to stay nearby so I could keep going to the same school. My friend Little Bill agreed that I could stay with him at his mom's apartment. He told me she was never around anyway. He told me not to call him Little Bill anymore though. He told me his name was just Bill now.

BILL

I soon learned one good thing about having a roommate with obsessive compulsive disorder is that they always keep the room clean.

I didn't even know Bill had OCD until the day I moved in and he pulled out this container of Lysol and a rag and started spraying shit down. I guess having lice made him worry about things being clean. His head wasn't shaved now. His hair was thick and red. He sprayed down the door and then he sprayed down the floor and then he sprayed down the place I was going to sleep—*SSSSS*. Then he took a rag and wiped it all down. He did this all over the walls. Then he sprayed the desk, the dresser, the closet door, the bed rails, and then the bed.

I told him I thought it was okay.

Bill just shook his head no. He wasn't listening to me.

He walked over to the side of the room and pulled out this giant plastic bag.

"What's that?" I said. Then he pulled out an orange pill bottle and sat it on the counter. Then he took out another orange pill bottle and sat it on the counter. Then he took out another orange pill bottle and put it up on the counter too. He took another and another and then he took out another five and put them one by one by one by one on the table until they were all lined up on the shelf like little soldiers. 1,2,3,4,5,6,7,8,9,10,11.

"What is this stuff," I asked again. Bill just smiled and told me that he was psycho.

Isn't everyone?

That's when "Dust in the Wind" started. He turned on his CD player and sat down on his bed and listened.

He said, "You like 'Dust in the Wind'?"

I said sure and started putting away all of my stuff that I brought with me. I tried not to think about Nathan or Ruby or graveyards.

I listened to the song: *I close my eyes, only for a moment and the moment's gone.*

Then Bill went over to the scale and weighed himself.

He weighed 225 pounds.

Then he got off and weighed himself again.

He weighed 225 pounds.

Then he told me the story of the Greenbrier Ghost.

THE STORY OF THE GREENBRIER GHOST

It was about this woman named Zona who suddenly died back in the 1890s. Her husband was so overcome with grief that he put a red ribbon around her neck and he buried her without letting the other women prepare the body. Weeks later her mother woke up and Zona's ghost was at the foot of her bed. She told her mother that her husband murdered her. He killed me, Mommy. He strangled me and broke my neck.

Her mother went to the sheriff and they exhumed her body. They found her neck was broken. It was just like the ghost said.

Then Bill told me it was the only case in the history of the country where a man has been convicted of murder on the second-hand testimony of a ghost. This story didn't cheer me up.

The song finally ended and he hit play again. *I close my eyes, only for a moment and the moment's gone.*

Then he went and weighed himself again.

He weighed 225 pounds.

There were other things Bill did too. He washed his hands. He took a hell of a lot of showers. He washed his hands some more. He sprayed some more Lysol. He weighed himself again. He weighed 225 pounds. He told me about the Greenbrier Ghost again.

Then he played "Dust in the Wind."

I close my eyes, only for a moment and the moment's gone.

I asked him if he had to listen to the song again. He said, "I thought you liked Kansas?"

I told him I was just being nice.

He turned it off. Then he started spraying the walls down with some more Lysol. "You'll see one day," he said. "You'll see." Then he played Kansas, *I close my eyes...*

So that night Bill told me what was wrong with him. He told me he had a condition called OCD.

A LIST OF OCD SYMPTOMS IN CASE YOU ARE A HYPOCHONDRIAC AND WONDERING IF YOU MIGHT BE SUFFERING FROM OCD:

1. Compulsive actions in order to alleviate anxiety.
2. Obsessive thoughts in order to alleviate anxiety.

3. A combination of compulsive actions and obsessive thoughts in order to alleviate anxiety.
4. Constant obsession with a particular repetition of actions/ and or thought patterns.

Then he told me how it happened.

He told me how he first knew something was wrong with him when he was ten years old. He was sitting up on the counter eating a giant bag of cheeseballs. He was covered in orange cheeseball dust. It was on his hands and it was on his fingers and it was on his face. He kept eating the cheeseballs and before long he started thinking that he was turning into a cheeseball too. All of a sudden his mother and brother came into the room and he started yelling at them: "Don't eat me. I'm a cheeseball. I'm a cheeseball."

So he jumped off the counter and before long he started running around because he thought they were trying to eat him. Of course, this freaked them out so they chased after him thinking that something was wrong. They chased him around the house. They chased him around again.

Then they chased him around the house one more time and now Bill was screaming, "I'm a fucking cheeseball. Don't eat me."

Then he told me about the Greenbrier Ghost.

And then he told me it was like this with chicken of any kind too. He cleared his throat again, *eeeeghh*. He told me if he got anywhere near chicken he would start to get all sweaty trying to swallow the thing. He told me about being a kid and trying to eat chicken legs. He would chew on it and have to spit it out. He couldn't bring himself to swallow it.

I said, "Damn."

He said, "I thought I was possessed by the devil for a while. I knew I wasn't in control anymore."

He said, "Then I realized no one is in control."

The next morning I woke up to the lyric:

I close my eyes, only for a moment and the moment's gone. All we are is dust in the wind.

I came home the next day, *I close my eyes, only for a moment and the moment's gone.*

I went to bed each night. *All we are is dust in the wind.*

I finally said, "Would you please stop it? Seriously. Stop."

He played, *I close my eyes, only for a moment and the moment's gone.*

STOP.

He grunted. He checked his weight. He weighed 225 pounds.

STOP.

He grunted. He checked his weight. He weighed 225 pounds.

He told me about the Greenbrier Ghost. *Back in the 1890s a woman named Zona suddenly died.*

STOP. You're driving me nuts.

He played his music.

When he was gone one day, I hid the CD.

He sprayed Lysol.

STOP.

He grunted. He rubbed his hands together.

He told me about the Greenbrier Ghost. *It's the only case in history where a man has been convicted based on the second-hand testimony of a ghost.*

STOP.

He sprayed Lysol and rubbed his hands together. He grunted, *errghhh.*

Then one morning I woke up and he was gone. He told me the night before that he was going to see his grandpa.

I didn't know what to do without him. I actually walked around and cleaned up. I felt a little fat. I got up on the scale and I watched the weight pop up. I weighed 196. Then I got down and rubbed my hands together.
I thought, *How much do I weigh now?*
I couldn't remember. I got back on the scale. I weighed 196 pounds. I got off. I got back on the scale. I got off. Then I went back to the closet and got out the CD. I put it in the player and pushed play. Then I started singing along, "I close my eyes, only for a moment and the moment's gone. All we are is dust in the wind." I listened to the whole song and then I did it again.
I close my eyes.
I listened to the whole song and then I did it again.
I close my eyes.
I told myself the story of the Greenbrier Ghost. *He killed me, Mommy. He strangled me and broke my neck.* I tried not thinking about Ruby and Nathan.

I listened to the whole song and then I did it again.

I close my eyes.

I told the story. *It's the only case in the history of the country where a man has been convicted of murder based on the second-hand testimony of a ghost.*

I listened to the whole song and then I did it again.

I looked down at my hands and my hands weren't my hands anymore. My hand wasn't made of flesh anymore. My hand wasn't even a hand anymore. I held it up and looked at it. It was orange. I said, "I'm a cheeseball. I'm a motherfucking cheeseball." I wasn't in control anymore.

I stayed up late that night and I thought about Nathan and how he died and I thought about my grandmother. I went through my wallet and looked at the funeral notice from a few months earlier.

I read:

IN MEMORY OF

NATHAN ELGIE McCLANAHAN

BORN
May 8, 1943
Backus Mountain, WV

PASSED AWAY
February 11, 1996
Beckley, WV

SERVICES
February 15, 1996
2:00 PM
Wallace and Wallace Chapel
Rainelle, WV
Pastor Steve Martin

INTERNMENT
Goddard Cemetery
Red Springs, WV

Then I went to sleep and I dreamed about graveyards.

AND THEN THE NEXT NIGHT

I dreamed about Ruby and she was telling me it's just one thing after another. Then she told me that some shit happens and then some more shit happens and then some more shit after that. There are floods, explosions, disasters, tornadoes and none of it makes any sense. It's all just one big joke you have to laugh at.

Are you laughing?

MESSING WITH BILL

I don't think we had anything to do after a couple of days living together except talk. Since Bill's mom was never around we sure as hell didn't go to school that much. No one could make us. For some strange reason we started talking about religion.

I started giving him hell about his views of homosexuality. He repeated again that it was an abomination of God.

I told him he was just pissed because he caught his cousin taking it in the ass one day. He came home early one day from school and there was his cousin getting fucked by the next door neighbor. I told him butt-fucking usually runs in families.

Then I reminded him about his silver-dollar-size nipples and how I didn't want him walking around with his shirt off when I was drunk because they kind of made me horny.

He grinned and just kept going on about homos being an abomination of God. Homos man, homos.

I asked him where he got that abomination of God thing from. He told me Leviticus. I asked him if Jesus ever said anything about homosexuality. I knew the answer was no. I told him didn't Leviticus also say you have to keep your woman outside the tent if she was having her period? That shut him up. Then he quoted Leviticus.

I told him that as much as he quoted the Old Testament you'd think he was Jewish.

Bill was getting mad.

I kept telling him seems to me if he loved the Old Testament so much we ought to change his name to Crookshankzowitz.

I told him yeah you're my Jewish friend Crookshankzowitz.

Bill was mad.

That morning I sat down at the computer and made a fake e-mail address that I could send him. The e-mail I made was called ourlordandsavior@hotmail.com.

I sent him an e-mail that went:

Dear Bill:

This is the lord. I have been listening to your religious conversations with your roommate Scott McClanahan. I would like for you to know that I am disappointed in your recent conversion to Judaism. It is a beautiful faith, and one my father started. But please understand that you must return to Jesus and the study of the New Testament or face eternal hellfire and damnation. Your friend and savior.

Jesus Christ.

The son of god.

P.S. Please quit skipping school so much. Remember, drugs aren't cool. Stay in school.

That evening Bill sat down in front of the computer and checked his e-mail. I watched over his shoulder. He scrolled through his e-mail and started reading it. Then all of a sudden he got up from his computer and walked over to me. He was halfway grinning, but he scratched his head and said, "Jesus just e-mailed me."

So Bill walked out of the room. I heard him praying in the other room.

I heard him praying for his grandpa and his uncles and then I heard him pray for my grandmother and me. I heard him praying for my Uncle Nathan. I heard him praying that my Uncle Nathan was in heaven. I heard him praying for a girlfriend. "I try to be a good person," he said. "But I'm very lonely. I'd really like a girlfriend to spend some time with. I'd just like to have someone who I could talk to. I know I'm not good-looking, but I would like someone." Then I heard him praying about his condition. He said he knew it couldn't stop forever, but he would like for it to stop for a day. He would like the voices and anxiety inside his head to stop for a day.

An hour or so later he walked back up to me and said, "I guess you think you're real funny, don't you?"

I didn't say anything.

He told me he was just pretending that I fooled him earlier.

It was around this time Bill started taking pictures of stuff. At first he bought the camera so he could take pictures of himself with his shirt off—flexing his muscles. And then he started taking pictures of other things.

He took pictures of trees.
He took pictures of flowers.
He took pictures of clouds.
He took pictures of his hands.
He took pictures of parking lots and trucks.
He took pictures of the Meadow River.
He took pictures of the sky and storms.
He took pictures of the mountains.
He took pictures of old civil war trenches.

I told Bill to take pictures of the dogshit outside the stray dogs were leaving all over the place but he refused.

Oh come on, Bill.

We watched the stray dog crapping outside the apartment. I begged him, please.

He still refused.

The next morning he was going on about the gays again and how it was an abomination of God. He went on about evolution and how he didn't come from a monkey. I tried to correct him and say Darwin didn't say that. He said we came from a common ancestor. He told me he didn't care. He told me it was an abomination of God and that there would be a lake of fire to burn it all.

I told him I came from monkeys. I was a wild animal.

So one weekend when Bill went home I decided I was going to mess with him some more. I had people who Bill knew come by. We went through Bill's drawer. Then we walked around and put his clothes on and we took pictures of each other.

And even better than that I took his camera outside too when he was asleep. The stray dogs were running around again. I went outside and saw these big piles of dogshit on the ground. The stray dogs had crapped everywhere.

I had an idea.

A week later Bill went to have his pictures developed. He stood in the middle of Rite Aid expecting to see pictures of his muscles and pictures of nature, but instead he found pictures of people he knew.

"Hey, it's pictures of my friends."

Then he noticed weird things about his friends. "I think it's pictures of my friends with my clothes on." Then he kept flipping and what did he see?

He saw trees.

He saw flowers.

He saw muscles.

He saw dogshit.

He saw giant piles of dogshit.

He saw giant piles of nasty-ass dogshit.

It was steaming dogshit that would burn into all eternity—as if the only thing that survived was dogshit. IT IS.

That night I dreamed my dream about Ruby and that the world was just one thing happening after another. I awoke and I saw that life was one big practical joke full of pain. Someone was laughing at us. Someone was torturing us. I remember being at Grandma Ruby's as a little boy and crushing the ants on her sidewalk. I saw all of Nathan's pain and I saw all of Grandma's pain explaining to relatives that Nathan was dead. "It's a debt we all have to pay."

Then she told me again, "Scott, Nathan is gone."

I told her I knew. I was there.

She sat in her recliner and she said again, "Scott, Nathan is gone. We have to find some way to carry on. We have our own debt to pay now."

We were ants and God was only a child with a nose full of snot. God was crushing the ants in the sun.

I left Bill alone for a few weeks. I didn't steal his camera. I didn't e-mail him from ourlordandsavior@hotmail.com. I didn't bring up religion for us to argue about. I didn't tell him to stop checking his weight. I didn't tell him not to tell me about the Greenbrier Ghost. Bill started going back to grunting and rubbing his hands together and playing his music. He stopped taking pictures of his muscles in the mirror. He went back to spraying Lysol.

Then one day Bill walked into class and asked me if I thought I was funny. I told him I didn't know what he was talking about. Then he told me about another e-mail I supposedly sent. It was supposedly an e-mail I sent pretending to be God.

He showed me the e-mail. It was from an e-mail address with nothing but zeros in it. 0000000@yahoo.com. It was an e-mail from God.

Dear Bill,

My son Jesus wanted me to e-mail you. I have to admit though that I'm pretty drunk. I don't know what to tell you about anything. I have to take medicine to go to sleep each night. I'm a sleepwalker. I know I wrote you to give advice, but now I see that I'm just complaining. I'm sorry to burden you, but I feel confused most of the time. I really don't know what I'm doing anymore. I know your roommate Scott made a toast to god one night when you were drinking 40 ounces. His toast went: Here's to God almighty, the laziest fucker I know. I want to tell you that it hurt my feelings. I know he recently lost his Uncle and is hurting, but I thought his toast was a bit rough. It hurt my heart.

I read how he wanted to tell Bill he wasn't lazy. He was just tired. He realized now it had all been a horrible mistake—the world. He knew he created not with any plan in mind. He created just because he felt so lonely—that was all. He was so lonely and now it was all out of his control. He said he was an atheist he realized, but only a true atheist believes in God. Therefore, maybe he wasn't an atheist because he didn't know if he believed in himself anymore. He said he was Peter Pan. He said he wanted something removed. He said he felt like a hermaphrodite.

Bill smiled and said he knew it was me. I got up and went to the bathroom. How could I tell him that I didn't write it? How could I tell him that maybe it really was from God. Maybe we would all meet in a lake of fire one day. Maybe we were all abominations. How could I tell him that I didn't write this e-mail, but the world was just a joke, and God was a lonely hermaphrodite who was writing e-mails to strangers in the dark? Who knows?

SO I WENT TO SEE GRANDMA

It had been months since Nathan's death and I wanted to see how she was doing. The first time I went to see her, she said, "Oh lordie, I'm dying."

The next time I went to see her it was, "Oh lordie, I'm dying." I always asked her if she liked living with Stanley and Mary, but she didn't say anything.

I borrowed Bill's car and I went to see her for a third time and it always happened like this.

I said, "Well, Grandma, I should get going."

Grandma told me there was no use to be running off.

Yeah, but I probably better get back. I have school in the morning.

Then it started, "Oh lordie. I don't feel no good at all." Then she started crying and said, "I think I'm dying all right."

My Aunt Mary came in and said, "Oh, Mother, you're fine. You're just upset that Scott has to leave."

Grandma said, "Hateful old thing walking around here like a bandy rooster. I don't feel good."

My Aunt Mary checked her pulse—"I don't know? Your pulse is really weird. Let me take your temperature."

She took her temperature and it was a little bit high.

So I agreed to take her to the hospital to be sure. I told her I had Bill's car. It was no big deal.

Mary told her, "You're just like the boy who cried wolf, Ruby—one of these days you're going to be really sick and we're not going to believe you."

My grandma told her she wanted them to know something. She wanted her to know that they might be taking care of her now, but she was still the boss around here. Little Nathan might be gone, and Little Scott might be living elsewhere, and she might be living at their house now, but she was still boss around here.

So I drove her to the hospital 40 miles away. I drove her through Danese and down the mountain. I drove her past our old house Elgie built out of wood from another house he bought for eight dollars. In the winter, the snow used to blow beneath the door. She told me about how Elgie used to hide his moonshine in the creek, but he was usually drunk when he did it. So when he returned he never could remember where he put it. She said there were still jars of his shine hiding in the mountains, waiting for us to find them.

We crossed the bridge and Ruby looked out across the river. It had been raining really hard that summer so the river was up and rolling all full of mud and roots.

So she looked out over the river and said: "Oh look out there. That river is nothing but a river of blood."

She repeated: "It looks like nothing but a river of blood and hearts."

So I took her to the doctor and she was telling me about how Nathan had missed her, and how he was crying at night and wanted her home, and how she knew he was waiting right now for her return.

Then I told her Nathan was gone.

She told me she knew.

I couldn't tell if she was losing her mind or just pretending to lose her mind.

I knew old people used the "losing my mind" excuse all of the time, especially if they were caught stealing at a grocery store.

And so we passed the place where the mountain caved in a couple of years before and killed her cousin who was riding along. I told her about how just a couple of weeks ago, I went through these old dusty volumes of Fayette County census records in the library—and I found her father and her mother, and that the first McClanahan in Fayette County was in 1872. She cussed to herself and said "shit" and she wanted me to know that she was from on top of Backus Mountain. She was a farmer's daughter and she didn't want to be associated with any coal-mining McClanahans who lived at the bottom of the mountain. She told me after Elgie's death his brother Jason called her and proposed marriage. Jason McClanahan was 80 years old. She said she had one McClanahan in her life and that was sure as shit enough for one lifetime.

When we got to the hospital the nurse took Ruby's vitals and said, "I think you're okay, Miss Ruby. It must have been something you ate."

Ruby raised her hands in the air and shouted, "Praise God."

Then Dr. Mustafa Mahboob came down and gave her an ass-chewing and told her that her family was going to put her in a nursing home if she didn't stop. He asked her if she knew how many times she had been to the hospital in the past two months. She shook her head no. He told her 10 times. He told her he knew she just lost her son, but she was out of control.

Then he told her Medicare was going to flag her. He told her she was going to get in trouble. I shook my head and nodded at her. So I put her back in the car and I took her home.

I drove up the mountain towards Prince and past all the old places. We drove past where Elgie sold moonshine and where Ruby used to wash her clothes in the river. And we drove past the old mine, which had a church in front of it now. She told me about how she used to sit on the front porch and blow a whistle when the cops were coming. She blew the whistle and screamed, "The revenuers are coming. The revenuers are coming." Then Elgie would hear her on the mountain and blow up the still.

She pointed to the hillsides and said, "There used to be houses all over."

Then she pointed to the side of the hill and said there used to be houses there too.

Then she pointed beside the creek and said there used to be houses over there too. There used to be houses anywhere you could put a house. She told me how Elgie brought home a box of dynamite from the river and tried to blow her up one day, but the dynamite got wet and wouldn't go off. She told me a revenuer disappeared one time. People said the McClanahan boys did it. She told me they tied him to a tree and put a shotgun in his guts. Then they fed him to a hog because hogs eat everything. This was called a coal camp. This was the true way of justice and truth and law.

And as we drove through the holler I could see the whole place. There was a moment when it felt like it was 1930 and I was traveling through time. I could see the mine. I could see people walking. There were houses everywhere.

It was all gone now. There were only mountains and a twisty-turny road with chug holes so deep you could bury your baby inside of them. For a while now you had to be careful because there was an abandoned mine shaft beneath the road. The state transportation officials were worried about the road caving in and cars falling down into this forever mine shaft. But now there was tall grass growing over everything and vines wrapping around old shacks and rusty railroad tracks and rickety bridges. There weren't any of the old places. There wasn't a coal mine. And there wasn't a house here.

And there wasn't…

And there wasn't…

There was only a train station nobody stopped at and the New River rushing all red and full of river mud.

When we got back home I helped Aunt Mary to get Ruby ready for bed. I told Mary that Ruby was fine. It was just indigestion probably. I helped put Ruby into bed. I touched her hand and told her I was going now.

"Oh lordie, I'm feeling horrible," she said. Then she clutched her chest. "I'm having chest pains." I kissed her cheek and I said, "I'll see you next week." She told me my grandfather Elgie used to have nightmares begging for the whistle to stop.

She wasn't dying.

She was lonely.

So I left and I heard Ruby shouting again, "Oh lordie, I'm dying." I didn't turn back. I wasn't sure we were even born yet. We were all inside of a giant mother right then and we were waiting to be born. Just like tomorrow, at dawn, we will be held in the arms of the giant mother. We will find warmth and maybe even war there.

I want us all to be ready.

SO NOW A REMINDER ABOUT THE THEME OF THIS BOOK AND ALL BOOKS

Tick, tick, tick, tick, tick…

I went back to Bill's mom's apartment, and it was all the same. It was just an apartment full of the…

CRAZY FUCKERS I KNEW

There was Reinaldo who always used to sneak into the bedroom and try on a pair of Bill's mom's crotchless panties. She moved out years before, but she still kept a pair of crotchless panties around. Bill used to get pissed and tell him to take off his mom's crotchless panties.

There was the foreign exchange student Tiertha Timsina who arrived in Crapalachia knowing only two words of English. Tiertha had to get married before he turned 18 or he would be sentenced by the wise men in his village to marry a tree. Lee told him, "I know if I had to marry a tree—I'd sure as hell put a lot of knot holes in it if you know what I mean. I'd fuck the hell out of that tree."

Tiertha and Bill bonded because they were both mountain boys. They talked about Sewell Mountain and the Himalayas and the elevations of the mountains of their birth.

We talked about the town of Lewisburg in the eastern end of the county and how we hated all the hippies who lived there who talked constantly about black bears and healing massage.

There was Six Toed Russell who snuck into bars and bet drunk lumberjacks. "Hey, I bet I have six toes on both feet."

The rednecks didn't believe and just said, "Whatever. The fuck you do." So Russell popped off his shoes and there they were. There were two feet. And there were, count them—1,2,3,4,5,6,7,8,9,10,11, 12 motherfucking toes wiggling around in all their glory. Russell was always good at math.

And then there was Naked Joe. Naked Joe used to run into people's yards and rip bushes out of the ground. "Fucking bush, I hate you."

One time an old lady said she was going to call the law. He better quit tearing up her shrubs.

"The law," Joe said. "Well you better tell your bush to quit talking so much shit."

But then that evening we sat in Bill's room playing Madden. Joe came into the room real quiet and then disappeared into the bathroom. A few minutes later he came into the room and stood behind us.

"Who's winning?" he said. He put his hands on his hips and said, "Man this game is getting good."

I felt something brushing against my back. I felt something sitting on my shoulder. I turned around and shrieked because right there was Naked Joe's dick sticking in my face.

I always wondered why people called him Naked Joe and now I knew.

Then there was Bill in the middle of it all. He stood around during our backyard wrestling bouts. He pointed to the mountains around us. He pointed to Beelick Knob and said, "That's Beelick Knob. Guess what its elevation is?"

Then he told us the story about the Greenbrier Ghost.

Then he pointed to another—"That's Shafers Crossing. Guess what its elevation is?"

But no one listened.

Then he pointed to another mountain and we didn't care again. Only Tiertha listened. He dreamed of his home in the Himalayas. But we didn't, even though Bill was telling us about where we were from.

He was telling us about our mountains.

Then Lee Brown stopped by.

LEE BROWN

Lee was 6'5" 275 pounds. He was 18. He came from a whole family of big people though. His older brother was 6'6" and his father was 6'7" and his little baby brother Dave was 6'5" and his mom was the itty bitty runt in the family. She was only 6'3".

Lee once drove all the way to Lewisburg just so he could sit in a trust-fund hippie restaurant and order a 15 dollar hamburger (raised without steroids or preservatives). He ordered, "Yes, I would like your 15 dollar hamburger but can I get it with the steroids and preservatives put back."

They refused and he shouted, "What the hell kind of restaurant are you running here?"

I thought these were the perfect examples of American youth.

So we hung out that evening looking through the phone book so we could make prank phone calls. Lee and I were looking through the phone book for names. Then Bill pointed out over the mountains and he told us about the elevation of the mountains. He told us about the Greenbrier Ghost. We weren't listening anymore because we were looking for names to call.

I looked up Ruby's old phone number. I wanted to call it and see if she would answer. Then Bill told us about Beelick Knob. He told us about Shafers Crossing. He told us about Sewell Mountain where his family was from. He told us about Stephen Sewell living in a tree, and running from the Shawnee through the rhododendron bushes before they finally caught and killed him in the woods. He was telling us about all of these places. He was telling us something important though.

He was telling about where we were from.

He was telling us about home.

OF COURSE

We were just looking for numbers to call. We called 438-6794, but no one answered. We called 438-5812 but then it was busy. We called 438-6494 but then Bill started whining again.

He said, "Guys, I don't think we should be doing this."

"Oh be quiet, crotchless panties," Lee said giving him hell yet again about the pair of crotchless panties.

"My mom does not wear crotchless panties."

It was true though. One night Reinaldo and Lee came out of the bedroom after they went through her drawers and Reinaldo was wearing the crotchless panties over his boxer shorts. It was true. Lee reminded him of this, but Bill just kept arguing.

"How do I know you didn't sneak crotchless panties in her drawer just to put them on that night—so you could make fun of me?"

Lee said: "Why in the hell would we want to take the trouble to sneak crotchless panties in here. I know you're sensitive about it, but it's not that big of a deal."

It was quiet for a second. Then he said, "Like I said it's not that big of a deal—crotchless panties."

Then Lee started giving him hell about his troll love. If it wasn't the crotchless panties—it was the fact he collected troll dolls.

Bill was famous for his troll love. One night a few weeks back Bill and Lee got into it. Lee said something to Bill about his mom's crotchless panties and Bill just flipped. He punched Lee harder than shit in the shoulder and so Lee started chasing him. They ran outside the apartment building. Bill was barefoot and bare-chested and only wearing Dallas Cowboy boxer shorts. It had been raining. He ran out into the rain and the muddy yard.

Lee was chasing him—and then all of a sudden... Bill... slipped... his feet went out from under him... the troll flew high into the air.

And then everybody moved in slow motion too.
RAAAAAAAAAA.
Bill fell into a mud puddle and the troll flew
Up
Up
Up
And then
Down
Down
Down a few feet beside him. And then in his slowed down motion picture voice—Bill shouted the words that made him famous. He reached and said from his mud puddle, "Save the Troll. Forget me."

I whispered to myself now, trying to give Bill hell. "Save the Troll. Forget me."

Then I stopped because Lee had already found another number to call—Junior and Shirley M. at 438-6494. He told Bill to do one. Bill didn't want to prank phone call them, but he did it anyway. Bill dialed the number. I picked up the other phone to listen. The phone rang on the other end and then somebody picked up. It was an old woman's voice.

"Hello," she said.

"Hello Aunt Shirley," Bill said.

"Yes," she said confused, and then I thought up something to say.

"Aunt Shirley, do you know who this is?"

On the other end it was quiet and then we heard Aunt Shirley shouting, "Praise Jesus. He's alive. Honey, it's little William. Billy, you've come back to us after all of these years. Billy, are you in trouble?"

Holy shit.

Billy?
What a fucking coincidence, I thought.

But then Bill just played along even though his name *really was* William. His name really was Billy. His name really was Bill. She was confusing this Bill with another Bill she knew.

"No I'm fine, Aunt Shirley. I'm just down here at the Pit Row." Pit Row was a gas station next to 7-Eleven.

He thought up a story to tell her. He came up with one quick and said, "I've decided to finally quit drinking firewater and come back home, Shirley."

On the other end we listened to Aunt Shirley crying out loud with joy. "Oh Bill, you've reached out to us, you've finally reached out to us."

So Bill started to pretend cry too.

But then he just kept going on: "Well Aunt Shirley, I'm down at P P P P P P Pits Row gas station." Then he started doing this stuttering thing.

"I'm down at P P P P P Pits Row gas station and I need somebody to come pick me up."

Bill took the phone away from his mouth and said: "Guys, we shouldn't be doing this. It sounds like she really misses this person she thinks I am."

I shushed him and so Bill started talking again. "Please, Aunt Shirley. Please come and get me. P P P P Please."

So Aunt Shirley whispered in the phone. "I'll get Junior and we'll come and get you. You remember Uncle Junior don't you? Of course, you were so little last time you saw him."

Then she didn't say anything for a long time, but then: "We'll be there in ten minutes."

So Bill started hanging up the phone and pretending to cry. "Okay, Aunt Shirley. Okay. I'll be waiting. I'll be waiting, Aunt Shirley."

And since Pit Row was just below Bill's mom's apartment—it was perfect. We looked out the window at the Pit Row gas station and waited on Uncle Junior and Aunt Shirley to show.

I just started laughing, it was so absurd. And then Bill said: "That was wrong of me to do. That woman thinks I'm someone she knows. She's coming all the way down here for nothing."

So we waited and waited. It wasn't about ten minutes later that this old rickety van showed up popping and cracking and popping into the Pit Row parking lot. Then the door opened. *BAM.* Then this big man in a cowboy hat stepped out and an old woman. She looked just like somebody's aunt. Lee watched them. I watched them too. They got out of the vehicle all fast and nervous and walked into the gas station. We watched Aunt Shirley walk around inside and Uncle Junior stood at the door smoking a cigarette. It looked like Aunt Shirley was talking to the guy at the counter. And then she walked out and looked at the pay phone on the outside. Shirley and Junior walked around the corner. Then Uncle Junior said something to her. Then Uncle Junior threw up his hands like whatever. "Where the fuck is he? That boy is nothing but trouble."

It was like she was begging him to do something. "I think they're leaving. I think they're leaving," I said.

And so they did.

Aunt Shirley didn't want to, but they did. Lee said: "We should wait awhile until they get back home and call again." And by this time Bill was starting to feel even worse about what we were doing. Bill wanted to speak up again and say they shouldn't be doing this, but by this time he was arranging his NFL collectible troll doll collection.

So Lee waited a half an hour and called her again. He handed the phone to Bill. Bill didn't do anything for a long time but then finally he said: "Aunt Shirley?" And Aunt Shirley sounded all out of breath and even more concerned, "Hey, where were you, honey?" We could hear Uncle Junior shouting in the background, telling her to put the phone down. He was telling her we were just punks messing with her—that's all. This wasn't her real nephew calling her out of the blue. Bill whispered to us: "What should I say?" And then he came up with something.

"Oh Aunt Shirley, I'm sorry. I had to go poop. I couldn't hold it anymore. I drank so much firewater and then the pooping started. It was horrible, Aunt Shirley." And then he said: "Aunt Shirley, will you come down here and get me again? I'm sorry. I'm so sorry. I promise I'll be here this time." I couldn't believe it. I could hear Uncle Junior shouting on the other line.

And then Aunt Shirley whispered she was sorry about what Bill had to go through. She was sorry that his parents got divorced. She knew the divorce was hard on him and his brother. She knew it was bad, but she wanted him to know that his parents loved him. She knew the divorce had a lot to do with his problems. She knew the kids teased him. She was sorry Bill's mom was never around.

It was as if she wasn't speaking about her Bill anymore, but our Bill.

And so Aunt Shirley showed up at Pit Row fifteen minutes later and parked the car. I watched her. Of course, Bill wasn't even looking out the window now. He was just sitting on the bed like he was stunned. He was sitting on the bed like he was scared. So Aunt Shirley got out of the car and walked inside just like she did last time. I watched her walk around the aisles and then I watched her asking the person behind the counter a question. She walked outside to the pay phone. She walked around the Pit Row gas station—once, twice, and then three times before walking back to the pay phone. She sat down on a sidewalk and waited. She waited and watched the cars passing by on the street. Then she waited some more—a half hour, an hour, two hours, three hours. It was dark. She put her hands over her eyes and buried her face in her fingers. She was crying. Bill said: "Someone should go out there and tell her we were just joking. Someone should tell her that she doesn't know me. She has me confused with another person."

But no one did. I just sat up in the window and watched her waiting. And she was still waiting there that night when we opened 40 ounces and drank them. She was still waiting there the next morning when we awoke. We started playing video games, and we didn't say anything to one another. Bill didn't say anything either. He acted like he didn't want to leave the apartment ever again—like he knew something no one else knew.

He knew there were two lives apportioned for each of us and there were families who we've never known who are out looking for us tonight. Even tonight they are out there searching for us. They are wishing to tell us who our true mother was. They are wanting to tell us who our true father was.

Listen: They are coming for us.

They are wanting to tell us our true names.

SO I WENT TO SEE RUBY AGAIN

I took her to the Methodist church she used to always go to. Usually she only went once a year. She went on Mother's Day because they gave a fruit basket to the woman who had the most children. Since Ruby had 13 children, she always won the fruit basket. Of course, she could care less about the yearly sermon, but she always liked the free apples and oranges. So I was surprised when she called and asked me to take her that Sunday. It wasn't Mother's Day and they weren't offering any prizes. I borrowed Bill's car and I drove her to the church.

I sat with her and listened to a sermon that went like this.

One time a man left home. He had argued with his mother and father the day before he left. They spoke horrible words to one another and he left without saying goodbye. He had been gone many years and even spent time in jail. Years later, he finally got out of jail and he wondered if his mother and father were even alive, and if they were ashamed of what had been said and of where he had wound up. He wrote to them and told them he would be coming home on a specific day the following week. If they wanted to see him and were not ashamed they should put a blanket on the clothesline, and he would know to come inside.

If the blanket was missing, then he would know that he was not welcomed. He would know to turn back. He told them he hoped they were in good health.

The man arrived by rail the next week. He was nervous when he stepped off the train. There was no one there to meet him. He walked up the worn path towards the home place and thought about the past. He thought about his time in jail. He thought about how ashamed his parents must have been. He thought about the horrible words they spoke. He was just about to turn around and go back to where he came when he saw a blanket in a tree. He kept walking and he saw another blanket. He kept walking and he saw another blanket. Then he turned towards home and the house was covered in blankets, the yard was covered in blankets, the clothesline was covered in blankets, the path to the door was covered in blankets. His parents were standing there and they were welcoming him inside.

*

I took Ruby home and she talked about Nathan. She talked about how she missed him. I didn't know this would be the last time I spent with her like this. I didn't know this last week would be the last week of her life.

RUBY'S END

A few days later, my Uncle Stanley called. He said they had to take Ruby to the hospital. He said that she was sick. So later that evening I went to see her. She acted like she didn't recognize me, but then she told me that the angel of death had come to see her that morning. She said the angel of death sat at the foot of her bed. She told me she heard Nathan's groans in her dreams. I heard Nathan's groans too. She told me the angel of death didn't say anything, but just sat looking at her. She told me that it wasn't a man or a woman, but it was the angel of death all right. She said that the angel was smiling at her. The angel had black teeth and I believed her. She wasn't faking her death. She was eighty years old and this was the end.

And so I stopped by my Aunt Mary's and told her that Ruby was real confused and she wasn't doing any good at all. I told her this was the end. I sat down on the bed and watched the cold rain beat against the windows. Then my Aunt Mary sat down beside me and said she didn't know whether to believe her or not. She didn't know whether she was sick or not because she was so good at manipulating you.

I looked at Aunt Mary and said, "I don't think she's playing this time. I don't think she's ever going over to the hospital again."

Then I felt myself repeating: "I think this is the end. I don't think there is ever going to be another trip to the hospital for her."

That night I stayed with my aunt and uncle. My Uncle Stanley came home the next morning at dawn and said they were sending Ruby home. He said the doctor came in and he just stood in front of her bed.

Ruby said, "Well it doesn't look good, does it, Doc?"

The doctoring man said, "No Ruby, it doesn't look good. I don't think there's anything else we can do for you."

Ruby said, "Well that's fine. I want to go home then. I want to go back to my real home then." The doctor signed the order and sent her home. He didn't send her back to Stanley and Mary's. He sent her back to the old house. The house where my father was born. There were cobwebs, but it was her home.

I went over there in the afternoon and she seemed so happy. She just sat up in the bed and smiled when I came in.

She said, "Well Nathan is gone, but he left me a good bed to die in. I keep thinking about the little feller."

I stood at the foot of the bed and I told her about all of my memories. I told her about how I remembered when I was a little boy and had the croup and she put the Vicks salve on my chest. I told her about how I remembered staying the night and how I stayed up looking at the baby dolls in the baby doll catalog with her. Then she smiled and said that she remembered it all. She had something to give me but she wasn't ready to give it to me yet. Then she smiled. She never got around to giving it to me. And now, years later, I just wonder what it was, what it was she wanted to give me…

WHO KNOWS?

I went back a couple of days later and she was dying. She was shaking and groaning and shaking.

For some reason I said, "Well you look good, Grandma," even though she looked like shit.

She wasn't eating. They had wheeled her around the house that morning so she could see her house and her things one last time. My uncle crushed her up a slice of orange and sat down beside her bed. Then he fed it to her. My grandma sat and looked like she was a little baby bird. That's what I thought she looked like. I watched my uncle feed his dying mother just like she used to feed him when he was a little boy.

I thought my grandma's face looked so much like Nathan's right then.

There was something about my Uncle Stanley's face too that looked just like my grandma's face from long ago. I wondered if my face would look like my Uncle Stanley's when I died. This was the story of faces. There was one face that looked like another face before it and then another face that looked like the face before it. This went all the way back until the beginning of time. Who knew what this face would look like a thousand years from now. Me?

There was a part of me that wanted it to be over. My Uncle Terry came in from California and sat beside her bed and said, "You gonna go see Nathan soon?"

Ruby whispered, "Yeah."

I shook my head and wanted it all to be over because I knew deep down inside that the dying and the dead were selfish.

I knew it that evening when my aunt said—"I know it's the wrong thing to say but I just wish it would all be over. I've got so much to do at work. I know that sounds terrible."

But I knew what she meant. Bill and Lee were going to drink beer on Friday and I wanted to drink too. I didn't want to disappoint them, and there was a part of me wishing she would just die. I knew that the dying were selfish, and the living were too.

I would have been all right if I would have just left it like that—if I didn't go back. But for some reason I did, and it was all a big mistake. I went back that Wednesday and the death rattle had started. She just looked gone, groaning full of death. And so I left that day thinking she wouldn't make it through the day. But she did. She made it through the day and then she made it through the next day. She kept fighting and fighting some more. I stayed at my uncle's the whole week. Then one morning I was sleeping when I heard the phone ring. It rang and it rang and I was awake all of the sudden. I heard my uncle's voice in the other room half asleep.

"Okay.

"She did.

"Okay."

And then he hung up.

My aunt went "Stanley" in this scared voice, but he didn't say anything back to her. He just went into the other room where my Uncle Terry was sleeping and he opened the door and told him.

My Uncle Terry said real quick like he was awake, like he was embarrassed to be sleeping, "Oh I thought she would. I thought she would."

Then he stood up and put his pants on.

They both got dressed and went into the kitchen. I got up and went into the kitchen and they were standing at the door. My uncle was the 7th son of a 7th son and my Uncle Terry was the baby of the family—a baby born blue who would have died if he hadn't been the first of her babies born in a hospital. I stood in my underwear and they stood in their coats and it was the strangest thing. Both of them just reached out and shook my hand. They shook my hand like they didn't know what to do. Their mother had just died and they were different now. They were free?

It wasn't until later that evening, when they were planning the funeral, that I heard how she died. My Aunt Bernice said that it was at 4 o'clock in the morning and she was in the back room folding clothes (Leslie and Bernice were staying at the house that night and taking turns taking care of her). She was folding clothes and then all of the sudden she heard a noise in Grandma's bedroom.

She listened and then Grandma said, "Good morning!"

So Bernice walked into my grandma's bedroom not believing what she heard. Grandma hadn't talked since Wednesday. After hearing Ruby say good morning, Bernice looked closer and Ruby was dead.

So after I heard about this, I just sat around and thought about what it meant. I didn't get drunk with Bill or listen to him talk about the Greenbrier Ghost or hang out with the crazy fuckers or make prank phone calls. I thought about how strange it was that somebody would say "good morning" and then die. I thought to myself that maybe this explained something about death. I thought maybe she was saying good morning to the angel of death who was coming back to get her now. I thought maybe it was the spirit of Nathan she was saying good morning to and he was taking her away. But then I thought that maybe it didn't mean anything. Maybe it was just the last little bit of oxygen escaping from the brain and it meant nothing. Maybe my Aunt Bernice didn't even hear her right. Maybe my Aunt Bernice made it up. Maybe it was just a groan of death that sounded like "good morning." And yet there was still something about all of this that said everything to me.

At the funeral the next day we all gathered around the grave beside Nathan's grave and Elgie's grave. My cousin's wife sang a song about how Jesus loves us, complete with backing vocals on a cassette tape. She keyed the tape to start, let her head drop down dramatically, and then she started singing. Then her daughter stood beside her and did the sign language for the song. She moved her hands together like it was a bird flying into the sky. She moved her arms to portray the waves. It was sign language. And there was something kind of funny about it because there wasn't one person who knew sign language there, but we all understood the signs. We were all deaf for a moment.

…So the preacher preached a eulogy about how Ruby waited to die. She took care of Nathan his whole life. And she never left him—even when people told her she should put him away in a home. She didn't leave him because he was her baby. At the end of it all, she waited until he died. She waited all those years until he died so she could die too. Then he said that blessed are the peacemakers, but even more blessed are the caretakers.

So just like at Nathan's funeral the Wallace and Wallace guy brought out a box of doves to fly away home and the preacher said, "We'll now release a dove which is a symbolic representation of Ruby's soul flying home to heaven."

And so they opened up the bird box and nothing happened. We waited.

And then this sleepy-looking dove just crawled out, except it didn't even look like a dove really but just a fat pigeon that somebody had painted white.

It had a look on its face like, *What the fuck? Seriously, people. What the fuck? It's way too cold to be doing this today.*

So the Wallace and Wallace guy tried to shoo it but it wouldn't shoo.

So the preacher repeated: "We'll now release the dove."

The Wallace and Wallace guy shooed it again. Finally the dove shot high up into the air and out and over our heads, but instead of flying away it just landed on top of this chain-linked fence. And so the Wallace and Wallace guy tried shooing it again and everyone giggled and gathered around in a circle throwing up their arms and shouting "shoo-shoo" at the bird high above. I shouted, "Shoo." We were all shooing.

But it wouldn't shoo.

And so it was.

I went back to Bill's mom's apartment. I had already missed too much school that week and I needed to go the next day. Bill told me he was going to skip again. I told him he was never going to graduate.

That night I dreamed that she didn't die. I dreamed she secretly escaped from the casket. I dreamed that she was back in Danese, WV, and she had kidnapped the devil. She was poking him in the ass with a pitchfork. She was stabbing him in the chest with the pitchfork, but there wasn't any blood and there wasn't any pain screams. There wasn't any agony. He was just whispering...

GOOD MORNING!

SO THE NEXT DAY

I went to school. I told myself I needed to start going to school and get out of this place. When I got home Lee and Bill tried to do something for me to take my mind off Ruby. We decided to have a backyard wrestling battle royale. Naked Joe wrestled Reinaldo. I wrestled Russell and busted a chair over his head. I was next matched with Reinaldo and he pinned me before losing his next match to Bill. Then we ended the royale with a no holds barred, winner take all against Lee. Whoever could get him down would win the backyard wrestling championship belt.

Bill got ahold of him by the neck and I got ahold of him by the legs and we tried pulling him down. Lee flipped Bill off of him. Reinaldo jumped on his back and Lee threw Reinaldo off his back as well. I was wrapped around his leg and he started walking around like I was a small child and he was my father giving me a ride. Bill jumped on his back again, but there wasn't any use. Lee flipped Bill off his back and threw me off his leg like he was kicking off a heavy boot and then he laughed and shouted: "Come on, ya little skinny bastard. Come on, you OCD bastard."

And we never could get him down.

We were all losers, but Lee was different. Lee was the greatest loser of us all and he could prove it because he was the owner of the backyard wrestling battle royale championship belt. He WAS our champion.

Then Bill looked up at the twilight time sky and told us about the Greenbrier Ghost. Then he told us how he was going to fall in love. He told us we should all try to fall in love too. He told us that love was his destiny. Then he pointed to the mountain and told us the elevation. He pointed to another mountain and told us its elevation. Then we all sat and dreamed about climbing to the top of them and looking down at the giant fucking hearts below, pumping full of blood and love. It was the destroyer of all things—this LOVE.

BILL IN LOVE

Of course, Bill had been in love before. One day he passed by a girl at school. She smiled at him and he thought he was in love.

That night he asked me, "You know that blonde girl at school?"

I said, "What?"

He said, "You know that blonde girl?"

I told him that really fucking narrowed it down for me. He told me that she smiled at him today and she smiled at him because she liked him.

I just shook my head and looked at him and then I told him just because a girl smiles at you doesn't mean she likes you.

He smiled and told me I was just jealous.

What the fuck?

That night he walked around the room and lifted his weights and flexed his muscles in the reflection from the dark window. He walked over to the mirror and rubbed his fingers through his thick red hair and said: "You know the girls like me because of my pretty red hair. They've all forgotten how my mother used to shave my head when I had lice."

Then he made a muscle. I pretended not to listen to him.

Then he rubbed his hands through his hair some more and said: "You're just jealous. You're just jealous because you don't have pretty red hair like me."

Then he flexed his muscles in the mirror and took his shirt off with his big red nipples showing. I told him once again not to walk around without his shirt on. I told Bill his Bill titties looked like girl titties if you looked at them right. I told him not to show them to the blonde girl or she might have to question her sexuality.

What the fuck?

The next morning he woke up and sat at his desk. He started copying something into a notebook. I walked towards him and looked over his shoulder. I saw a *W W W* and then another *W*— all lined up in a row. He was writing *W*'s?

I said: "What are you doing?"

Bill said: "I'm practicing my *W*'s."

I said: "Why the hell are you practicing *W*'s?"

Bill said girls like guys with good penmanship.

What the fuck?

The next day he wrote a poem. It took him hours. That evening he wanted me to read the poem he wrote. He handed me the poem and I read it.

I read: "Oh my love/my darling. I hunger for your touch a long, lonely time."

At first it seemed familiar, but I kept reading. "And time goes by so slowly and time can do so much."

It was "Unchained Melody."

I said, "It's 'Unchained Melody.'"

Bill said, "No it's not."

I said, "Yes it is. You just wrote down the lyrics to 'Unchained Melody.' That's not a poem, that's just writing down lyrics."

He said, "No I didn't."

But he did. Then he started humming the song and I could see that he was different. He was different because he meant these words and his eyes said, "Where to? What next?" Then his mouth said the saddest word in the world: "Tomorrow."

What the fuck?

BUT HE NEVER LOVED ANYBODY LIKE HE LOVED...

JANETTE

I didn't know it then, but the poem was for her. Janette was this tall girl who lived in the apartments behind the gas station. You could see the door to her house from our bedroom window. She cleaned houses after she quit school and took care of an old woman who lived in the apartment next door. One day she made the mistake of saying hi to Bill when she passed him in the alley. She was being nice to him. She wasn't ignoring him like everyone else and that's all it took. Bill came in and told me Janette said hi to him. Bill told me he was finally in love. He told me that lice business was all behind him now and a girl liked him.

He even called up his grandpa on the telephone to tell him he was courting this girl. I sat on the bed beside the phone and listened to him talk to his 90-year-old grandfather.

"Hey, Paw," he said. "Hey, Paw. How you doing?"

Grandpa couldn't even hear at all so Bill started shouting at him louder.

He said, "Hey, Paw. I'm courting this girl." He stopped. "Yeah, I'm still going to school."

I laughed to myself at his use of the word *courting*. Bill saw that I was laughing at him. He laughed too but he kept right on talking.

So I said, "*Courting*, Bill? Are you serious? It's no wonder you can't get any pussy."

Then I stopped laughing because I wasn't much better off. I wasn't getting any pussy either.

Then Bill looked up Janette's mother's last name in the phone book. I asked him if he was seriously calling her after only saying hi to her. Bill didn't answer me. He just dialed the phone.

He waited. He said, "Hey, Janette. This is Bill."

And then there was quiet but he kept going.

"This is Bill. You know the guy with red hair?"

"No. Red hair. That's right." He was quiet. "Oh, you said hi to me today."

Then Naked Joe came in and asked what we were doing.

I told him Bill was calling Janette.

Naked Joe said, "What the fuck? You can't do that."

Joe went over and started eating a bowl of our cereal. He just laughed and said, "That's real great for a guy who asked Fat Jimmy to suck his dick."

I asked him if he just came over here to eat our food.

Naked Joe said he was hungry. I told him to get the hell out of here. He finished eating his bowl of cereal and then he went home.

She still didn't know who Bill was. He still asked her though. "Well I was just wondering if you want to do something tomorrow?"

The voice on the other line was talking.

Then Bill said, "Yeah with me. That's what I meant. You want to do something with me tomorrow?"

She told him she had something to do the next day. He said, "Well okay, thanks."

He panicked.

He hung up.

It was like he was thinking about Fat Jimmy again.

He was wondering if it was true.

A few months before, Bill got so drunk Lee had to ask Fat Jimmy to help carry him up to the apartment. Fat Jimmy was a big black guy who worked across the street at 7-Eleven. Lee messed with Bill the next day and told him that he asked to suck Fat Jimmy's dick. Lee said Bill opened his eyes and looked at Jimmy. He told us Bill said, "Fat Jimmy, you want me to suck your ding dong. I'll suck your ding dong, Fat Jimmy."

When Lee told us that he laughed and said, "Man it made me uncomfortable as hell coming up the stairs like that and you offering Fat Jimmy sexual favors. Here Jimmy is just trying to help you out by carrying your drunk ass up the stairs and here you're trying to seduce him. I think it made Jimmy uncomfortable too." Of course, Bill freaked out and started to question his sexuality.

So now Bill was asking me again: "Do you think I really asked Fat Jimmy what Lee said I asked him?"

"What do you mean?"

"Ask Fat Jimmy what Lee said I asked him about."

I told him not to worry about it. We were all gay when it came down to it. Bill didn't say anything.

Then the next night—he picked up the phone again.

He said, "Hey, Janette. This is Bill Crankshanks."

There was quiet again. He kept going. He said, "Yeah this is Bill. Yeah. The guy with red hair who called you yesterday."

Then he asked her the question again.

"You want to do something tomorrow?"

She told him the same thing as the day before. He still didn't know what this meant.

He didn't know this meant no.

He said, "Well what about the next day?"

It was quiet.

Then Bill said. "Oh that's okay. What about the day after that?"

She told him that was Valentines Day.

So Valentines Day rolled around. Bill got this idea to get her some flowers. He was going to leave them on her door and surprise her. That evening I was going to take some books back to the library and Bill followed me down with the flowers he bought. When we got outside the wind was blowing. Leaves were blowing across the yard, and the wind was kicking up like hell. I even flipped up the collar of my jacket. Bill stood below the locust tree watching me walk away. Then he said, "Scott— do you know which door it is? I can't tell from down here. You wanna go with me?"

I turned around with my books in my hands and said, "It's just down there."

Then I stood for a second…

Naked Joe was standing outside smoking a cigarette. He told Bill that he heard Janette was a party girl. Bill didn't say anything. I told Joe to shut up, but he kept going. Then Joe told him that he bet he could go there tonight and get a blow job.

I told him to shut up again. Bill didn't say anything, but just walked down the alley with his flowers. He was going to give them to her. Then I stood for a second and asked. "You want me to go with ya?"

Bill thought it over. "No. I'll be all right."

So I said okay and just turned around and started walking off to the library, but then I started feeling bad.

I turned around and told him to give me the flowers.

Then we turned and walked towards Janette's. On the way down there Bill lost his nerve and decided to wait awhile.

"I think I'm just going to wait," he said.

I told him not to be nervous. He told me he wasn't nervous, but when I looked his hands were shaking. So I went off to the library.

It was an hour later when I got back that Bill finally got his nerve up and went to put the flowers on Janette's door. Of course, by this time everybody was hanging out of Bill's mom's apartment chanting for him.

Bill, Bill, Bill.

So Bill took off through the darkness running like a burglar up on his tiptoes across the grass. He finally set the flowers down on the door of her apartment. And then he took off running the other way without realizing he set them down on the wrong door and had rung the wrong damn doorbell. He was so nervous he put them on the wrong door.

Lee was shouting to him out the window: "No, Bill. No. It's the wrong door."

He couldn't hear us though. He just thought we were cheering him on, so he ran all the way back to us.

By that time the person who lived in the wrong apartment took them inside. So Bill had to go all the way back down to the wrong apartment and ask for the flowers back.

He knocked on the door. The door opened. He was talking. Then he had the flowers again. He put them beside the right door this time. He rang the doorbell.

Then I heard Lee whisper: "Look at that crazy, beautiful bastard."

And when Bill got back upstairs, he called Janette and asked her if she had got them.

She said thank you—she did.

That night he couldn't stop smiling. He sat in his bed and we drank beer and he told me about Scotland. He told me about how he dreamed of going to those mountains, how the mountains of Scotland looked just like the mountains of home. Then he talked about his family.

There was Uncle Dan, and the old man, and Jay, and Bill's dad Butch who never crossed bridges. If he had to go somewhere it might take him days because he never would cross a bridge. He thought bridges were bad luck.

Bill's Uncle Dan was agoraphobic and manic depressive.

Bill also said he was a little bit schizophrenic. That was actually a diagnosis a doctor in the army gave him. "He's a little bit schizophrenic."

This was about the time Dan decided he needed to go and save President Carter. He started hearing all of these voices telling him that President Carter was in trouble and Dan was the only one who could help him. He was the only one who could save Carter from the demons and those motherfucking devil worshippers. He gave the demons and the motherfucking devil worshippers a name. He called them Republicans.

Of course, Dan hadn't been out of the house for two years before this. Two years before he parked his red Chevy beneath an oak tree. He went inside and didn't come out again until the very moment he decided to go and save Carter. The oak tree was hundreds of years old.

This car had not been moved since Dan went inside that day so long ago. But now he came outside, started the car, which started on the fourth try, and he took off. Then after he took off, the tree which had stood for hundreds of years, fell over, *TIMBER*, and landed right where the car would have been sitting. No one got hurt, but the tree came crashing down, like it was not the roots that had kept it up, but the car. It was proof that it was good luck when the hallucinations came. It was always good luck to listen to the voices inside your head and do exactly what they said.

So Dan took off down 81 to save President Carter. A police chase ensued. He ended up wrecking nine police cars. After he wrecked nine police cars they took him into this jail cell in some town. It was a county jail with a row of cells in it. Dan was all hopped up and manic. It was like he had super human strength. He went over and took hold of the sink and ripped it out of the wall. They took him out of that jail cell and put him in another one. He took hold of the sink in that cell and ripped it out just like the other. He finally ripped out another before the cops decided it was a good idea to handcuff him to the bed.

After that, they put Dan at the state mental hospital in Weston. He had been there for six months before he was allowed visitors for the first time. So the old man who always cooked for the boys spent three whole days frying chicken, mashing vats of potatoes, and cooking a giant chocolate cake. It was enough food for ten people. But he cooked it anyway.

The old man never spoke, and he never cussed. If you asked him how he was doing he would just nod his head yes. If a carpenter came into his lumber supply business and asked for a particular type of wood, the old man would just walk over to where it was at and show him. He never said a word, and he never cussed. Not a *shit*, not a *damn*, nothing.

So they took the food to Weston and called for Dan at the front desk. They were going to have a picnic outside. When they called Dan instead of just coming out by himself, he started waving for all of the mental patients to follow him. "You want some food? You want some food? You want some food?" The patients at the West Virginia State Mental Hospital in Weston answered with a resounding yes. So here he came with an army of crazy people behind him. There was a fat woman there. She picked up the whole cake and ate it in three or four bites. Her face was covered in chocolate cake.

The old man didn't say anything to her. The old man didn't say anything when they told Dan goodbye. He didn't say anything when he drove all the way back home. He didn't say anything when he pulled into the garage, but then finally he said something. He finally walked into the house and he said completely calm, "That fat bitch at the mental hospital ate my whole goddamn cake."

Of course, Bill was still hopped up about Janette as he was telling me these stories. He was still sitting in his fake kilt without his shirt on and watching *Braveheart* on the VCR. I even caught him mouthing the last words of the brave warrior William Wallace. "Freedom."

I asked him if he just said "freedom," but he denied it. I asked him why he was wanting to watch this crap movie again and why he was putting a towel around his waist like a kilt? He told me that Janette would love him now.

He told me he was going to move to Scotland with Janette.

Then he watched the movie some more and mouthed the word again. *Freedom.*

I didn't tease him about anything because he was happy that night, but then he started talking about his dad Butch.

Butch had the biggest head you've ever seen. He wore an adjustable cap, but the cap was always on the last ring and about to pop from his giant pumpkin head.

The first time his dad lived away from the mountain he was working in a sawmill that was about an hour away. One day he was off so he decided to walk to the post office. It was winter time and there was ice all over everything. Butch was wearing flip flops and he ended up breaking his face. He started walking down the steps of the post office and there was some frozen water on the steps. He slipped and fell. But as he was falling he looked up and there was one of his flip flops going end over end up uP UP into the air in slow motion. It went so far up that it landed on top of the post office. He broke his jaw and his cheekbone and he knocked out a couple of teeth. He broke his goddamn face.

So Butch walked back to his apartment and called the old man. He said, "Pa, I just broke my face. I think I need help. I think I need you guys to come here and help me and take me to the emergency room."

The old man was real calm and said, "Well that's okay, son. It's a bit late to be driving. We'll be down tomorrow to get you."

His son just broke his face, and lived only an hour away, but the old man said he'd be there in the morning to get him.

Then Bill and I laughed and said we should go to the post office and find the flip flop and return it to his father. We imagined it still sitting there after all of these years, on top of the post office and just waiting to be worn. We knew the foot who walked with it would finally walk free.

Then Bill laughed. He said—they weren't gone from us. There are no such things as ghosts, because they do not haunt us. He told me Ruby was not gone from me. He told me Nathan was not gone from me.

They are here right now.

They are holding our hands and whispering a whisper we will whisper one day. They are whispering—FREEDOM.

FREEDOM?

But then the next morning Lee came over to the room and woke Bill up.

He said: "Bill, get on up and look out the window—it's Janette."

I got up and looked out the window and I saw what was happening. It wasn't good. It was Naked Joe. I told Lee, "No, let him sleep. Don't tell him." Lee kept shaking Bill awake. Bill got up though and went over and looked out the window, down towards Janette's apartment. And what did he see, but Naked Joe giving Janette a kiss and leaving her apartment. She was reaching into Joe's sweatpants and rubbing his dick. Then they were laughing. He'd spent the night with her. Bill just sat there looking out the window for what seemed like the longest time, not saying anything.

It was as if he was seeing our families from the past cross those lonely oceans to live in mountains, and as they crossed that ocean—it wasn't the word *freedom* they were whispering. There was only one word they were whispering now, a word we will whisper one day too, *oh SHIT!*

JANETTE PART 2

So Bill started losing all kinds of weight after Janette. It was like a whole new Bill. There was an FB time in Bill's history and then SB time. Fat Bill and Skinny Bill. He looked like one of those bobbing head dolls with his big head and this skinny body.

I turned around one day and he looked different.

"Goddamn," I said.

He went to school in work clothes with about four t-shirts or so beneath it. For lunch and dinner all he ate were peanut butter sandwiches. He ate a peanut butter sandwich for lunch, and a peanut butter sandwich for dinner. On top of that he drank 9 glasses of water and that's what started it.

I sat in school and I read about how everything changes even in Crapalachia. I read about how the miners became machines, and the loggers became the machines and the tiny roads turned into interstates and the towns became fast food drive thru's and gas stations and the people became people to serve tourists and let the tourists laugh at their accents.

I read about how people charged money to take people down the river. They charged people money to go mountain climbing. The people worked in restaurants so that tourists could laugh at their accents. They were paying for something that was given for free. The people from here didn't have to run a river to prove that it existed. They didn't have to climb a mountain just to climb it. It was enough that the river was a river and the mountain was a mountain and inside of them were mountains too.

In the evenings, Bill sat and talked about how people hurt one another. He talked about how he heard voices sometimes and how hard it was to think the same thing over and over. I asked him if he ever thought about suicide. He said, "Yeah." Then he asked me if I ever did. I said, "Every fucking day."

The next morning Bill started checking his weight all of the time. He brought in this scale and sat it on the floor. In the mornings he got up and walked over to the scale. Then he stood up on the scale. Then he checked his weight. He got down off the scale and walked back over to his bed. Then he got a drink of water. Then he walked back over to the scale. He stood up on the scale again. He checked his weight. Then he did it all over. He did this all the time—50 times a day.

We went to school and he went over to the cafeteria and instead of eating a sandwich, and a salad, and a hamburger like he used to eat, now all he did was eat a peanut butter sandwich and drink 9 glasses of water. He was always drinking water. He drank one right after the other until he had filled his stomach up. It was something else to watch, him drinking all that water and getting all grumpy and mad.

Then we went into class and we read about The Greenbrier Ghost, we read about the Hawk's Nest disaster. We read about how our place was changing. I read about the Sago Mine disaster and the men who survived an explosion only to have so little oxygen left they all went into the corner of the mine shaft and hid behind a giant rubber curtain. The giant rubber curtain was supposed to protect them from carbon monoxide. They put on the breathing mask, but there was only an hour of air left. They spent what time they had left writing letters to their children and wives. The letters went like this:

Tell all I'll see them on the other side.

It wasn't bad. I just went to sleep. I love you. Jr.

Your daddy didn't suffer.

After Bill lost all the weight his personality really changed. It seemed like any little thing that happened would just set him off. One night in the room he was bitching and complaining about how something was wrong. Bill and Lee started getting into it.

Lee said something that pissed Bill off and then I shook my head and said: "What the hell happened to you? This new skinny Bill is pissed off all the time. I want fat Bill back."

He started looking out the window all of the time. He kept looking down to the building where Janette lived. He did this once, and he walked away. Then he did it again, and then he walked away. He did it a million times.

"Seriously, Bill. Fuck," I said. "She's going to see you looking out the window so much you're going to freak her ass out."

He did it again.

Then we went to school and we studied the past. We learned about how rescuers went into the Sago Mine and found the miners. They were still alive. They were all alive. CNN reported all miners found alive except one. WVU won a football game that night. The governor said it was a night of miracles. There was a mistake made though. The radio wasn't working properly. They weren't alive. They were all gone. They were all dead except one. His name was Randal McCloy. He was a young man in his 20's with a young wife and two children. It is believed he survived because the rest of the men in their 50's made the decision to share their oxygen with the younger man, and keep him alive for his young wife and small children.

The young man watched the older men go to sleep one by one. And then it grew quiet.

And then Bill was up in the room that evening, and had his shirt off doing some kind of sit-ups. It seemed like every week after Bill lost his weight he would bring in some new kind of fancy sit-up machine. He would have the Ab Cruncher 100 or another one called the Ab Buster 3000. Or he would be down on the floor doing crunches as fast as he could 1,2,3,4,5,6,7,8… And he counted them off with his face all covered in sweat.

Then he stood up and said: "Whelp that's another 500 crunches."

Then he went over to the wall mirror and looked at himself and flexed his muscles. Then he looked out the window again.

Of course, after a while this really freaked Janette out—this guy looking out the window down at her apartment everyday, watching her leave for work. So I guess she had enough and ended up calling the cops.

The cop came by that afternoon and said there were complaints about Bill looking out the window and staring. He said Bill wasn't in trouble yet, but the young woman was afraid. I told the cop it was all right. I told the cop Bill suffered from OCD.

The cop said, "What?"

I told him it would be okay.

I told him Bill wouldn't do it anymore.

That evening when I came back to the room Lee and Bill were unfolding a sheet all the way out. They got up on two chairs and they took some clothespins and hung this sheet all the way over the window. We had this giant sheet across the window so Bill wouldn't be looking out the window and freaking Janette out. It made the room dark as hell. Of course, Bill would still go over to the window and peak out the corner every now and then. Whenever I wanted to go look out the window I had to pull the sheet back too. It was like this for 4 months.

Then one day Bill came in and told me he didn't care about Janette anymore because he had a new girl now. He just came back from a date with her. He told me they went to the movies. He didn't say if it was a girl from school or not.

"Did you kiss her?" I asked.

He told me, "Well with it being a first date and all."

I asked him what movie they went to see.

He laughed.

He couldn't tell me.

I didn't ask him what her name was because he wouldn't be able to tell me that either.

He just went over and sat in his chair in front of his desk. He turned on his music and he started practicing his *W*'s. *I close my eyes…*

So now when I think about Bill I always think about him holding the flowers for Janette. I think about that Valentines Day. I still see him standing outside the apartment. And it's dark and I have books in my arms taking them back to the library. Bill's just standing in front of the bushes with the flowers in his hands. And the wind's blowing so hard Bill's head of red hair is all tussled. I see myself putting the collar of my coat up and just watching him.

He's saying, "Do you remember which door it is, Scott?"

I see him standing there and his flowers are blowing over in the wind.

So I added Bill's name to the list of people I have ever loved. I wanted to write down these names so that I can remember them one day when everyone else has forgotten. I wanted to write a list of all the people I had ever known and keep them in my heart. I wanted to have a list of them even though I couldn't see their faces.

THIS LIST BEGINS...

Gary McClanahan, Audrey Karen McClanahan, Audrey Karen's story of her family, Nell Jones, Samantha the dog, Nanook the dog, Midget the dog, Razy the cat, Buddy the dog, Iggy the cat, Stanley, Stirley, Leslie McClanahan, Aunt Bernice, Aunt Mary, Monte and Lisa, Uncle Larry, Aunt Mary Ellen—the most beautiful woman I knew, her children, Mary the cleaning lady, Lil Bill, Big Bill, Elgie McClanahan, Russell Wilson, Mickey Hawkins, Mike Chapman, Wayne Tiller, Brent Sanford, Jason Taylor, Jay Lilly, Ricky Duggan, Nicole Owens, Ammie Costa, Reinaldo Lopez, Keith Cordial, Jenna D, Chastity Burns, Tracy and the Fury's, Keith and Eric Fogus, Carl Taylor, Robbie Bragg, Ulysses Phipps, Chad Tabor, and church: Joyce Hanshew, Melvin Hanshew, Ada and Harold Sifers, Ruby Hanshew, Harold Hanshew, George and Lena Deitz, Blaine and Aline Cook, Blaine Duncan, the Gwinns, Gary Redden, Charlie and Janette Redden, Viven and Ruth Bragg, the football team: Joey Fitzwater, Bill Bob, the baseball team: Boozy, Aaron Brown, Ryan Crookshanks, Kim Maguire, Mandi Demoss, the people at law school I secretly hated, Charlie and Dan, Ja Ja, Tom Maguire, Arlene Maguire, Chris Oxley, Lisa Griffin, Tim Keenan, Colin Worthington, Tammie Toler, Karen Angle, Jo Price, Sherry

Koon, Mrs. Walker, Kenny Walker, Charlene Green, J.C. Dunbar, Patti Milam, Coach G., Casey Whitlow, Dr. David Bard, Dr. Baker, Dr. William Ofsa, Rosalie Peck, John Turner, Aunt Lynn, Mark, Marz Attar, Tom Attar, Carrie Sanders Turner Ricks Attar Sanders, Wood and A, Tia and Fay, Sue Sanders, Sarah Turner, Sarah McClanahan, Iris Grace McClanahan, Samuel Ray McClanahan.

These are the names that are written inside my heart, but my heart will die one day. So I want these names to stay inside this book forever, but if this book is needed for fire, then set this book on fire. Then these names will live inside the other names, inside the invisible ashes. There is enough fire burning inside my secret heart to keep them warm for a long time.

If you recognize any of these names from this book, please write to me, or better yet. Come quick. Tell me they have returned. Tell me they are alive and living well.

And I will tell you something else.
I will tell you that you have been visited by ghosts.

I know there will be other love names to add to these present names. The lovely Eleanor Gould.
They are out there. I am wanting to find them.
I am searching for you.

THE BREAK IN

So Bill did something stupid. A few nights later he was so pissed off he broke into the school. He took a sledgehammer and busted through the walls. He busted a hole in the wall of the cafeteria and stole a whole box full of salt and vinegar potato chip bags. He emptied chalk dust in the hallway and pissed in the chalk dust. The school was wrecked.

The principal went into her office and sighed because she thought her office was left untouched. None of her papers were messed with and none of her filing cabinets were turned over. This was different from the other rooms. She even asked the secretary, "Why would he trash the rest of the school and leave my office alone?" The secretary just shook her head because she didn't know either. The principal sat down at her desk to call the police and the superintendent's office. She opened her desk drawer. She reached in for the phone book. And then she screamed. She screamed because she saw a big turd sitting perfectly in the middle of her desk drawer. Someone had crapped it there.

"Damn, that's cold to shit in somebody's desk drawer," Lee said.

I told him this was different though. This was not your ordinary robber. This was a robber who actually took the time to shut the drawer afterward. Most people would have left the drawer open and took off, but this guy was different. This guy was something of an artist.

We found out that Bill had been arrested that afternoon. The police asked me if Bill had been home last night. I told them I didn't know. The police went through the numbers of absent students for the day and when they went by Bill's mom's apartment they found him asleep on the couch with five or six empty salt and vinegar potato chip bags sitting on the floor.

There was only one thing to learn from this.

The world was a weird world.

The world was a joke.

Oh well.

I WENT BACK

So I tried not to think about Bill over the next couple of weeks. I went to school and I studied. They sent Bill away to juvie because he wasn't an adult. I came home to Bill's mom's apartment in the evenings and I studied. I thought about Nathan and I thought about Ruby and I thought about long ago. I thought about long ago so much that I wondered if they were really dead.

But she was dead. I knew she was dead when they all showed up at Ruby's house over the next couple of months and started gathering up all the stuff they wanted. There was somebody who wanted the pictures (half of them were gone already). There was somebody who wanted the dolls. There was somebody who snuck out the back door with four garbage bags full of stuff. There was my cousin who bought the bed off my uncle and paid for it a couple months later—COD. We watched the rest of them go inside and gather up all the things they wanted in garbage bags. We watched people pull pickup trucks to the front door and fill them full.

Stanley just sat and watched them all and said, "It's like a bunch of damn vultures. It's like a bunch of damn vultures licking a bone clean."

Of course, we got something too, but we didn't call ourselves vultures. A couple of days earlier, I told my uncle that all I wanted was Nathan's checkerboard. And so the day after the funeral, my uncle came home holding the checkerboard and said, "Here."

It was my Uncle Nathan's checkerboard, all beat up and taped together in the middle. I sat and ran my fingers over the checkerboard and I thought about ghosts.

After it was all done, I saw them again. One night I dreamed we were all back at Grandma Ruby's and we were all sitting around the table in a big circle. Grandma was in her recliner in the kitchen, talking and ordering people around just like always. Then the rest of the family sat around in a circle, except there wasn't any table now. Then all of the sudden this man walked in. It was Nathan. At least it looked like Nathan. He was taller and he had a beard. And it was like he had never even suffered from cerebral palsy.

Everybody was like, "You're walking. You're walking."

He walked around the circle, and he shook our hands. He shook my Uncle Terry's hand. And then he shook my Uncle Stanley's hand. And then he shook my hand. And that was the thing about it. He wasn't like I remembered him at all. He was all different now.

He was fucking angry.

I found a video my Uncle Terry made of my Grandma Ruby's last days. I'd been watching it for weeks now. On the side of it he wrote Ruby Irene Goddard 1917-1997. And so I pushed play and watched the video of my Grandma Ruby in her deathbed, all broken-looking and little. And my Uncle Terry was sitting beside her bed and she was dying.

I started hanging out with this girl Charity. She was over at Bill's mom's apartment one night and I asked her if she wanted to watch this video.

"What is it?" she asked.

"Oh it's this video of my grandma dying."

She shook her head. "Fuck no. That's weird." Then she asked me if this was my idea of being romantic.

So I went back. I took Bill's car and I took Charity and I drove down to the old house. As I drove up the road I swore I was going to see the house again just like I always saw it. I swore I was going to see the house from far away with its lights on, glowing golden in the night. I swore I was going to see blankets covering the trees and leading up to the door. I wondered if it was going to be like this—if I was going to see the front door open and the screen door closed like in the summertime, and I wondered if I was going to be able to see everything inside the house—Nathan sitting at the head of the table and Ruby hobbling around on her old cane. I wondered if I would see myself from years earlier walking around as well. And that's what I expected driving by Grandma Ruby's house in Danese.

But as I drove closer to the house, I realized there wasn't anything like that anymore.

THERE WEREN'T ANY BLANKETS.

There was just the house and it was all locked up and alone. And it was all boarded up too and there weren't any lights on anymore. And so I looked to see Nathan sitting at the table but he wasn't there. And then I looked to see Ruby hobbling around and cooking chicken and gravy on the stove, but she wasn't there anymore either. I stopped imagining it all because Ruby was in the ground now.

I walked with Charity around the house and found an unlocked door, which I opened and went inside. I felt like a burglar. And it was strange.

It was so empty inside. It looked so empty and broken down. There was the smell of musty carpet in the air and grooves in the floor from where the furniture sat for years. I walked with Charity into where Nathan always leaned against the footrest when he watched *Walker, Texas Ranger*. And then I walked her back into what they called Terry's room. I saw that the ceiling was falling and water stains were running down the walls and so I said that it was just an old thrown-together place that didn't even have a foundation really. Now it was falling down. It wouldn't take long before it would all be gone.

I went into the kitchen and there was an old box of tapes on the floor. It was full of Nathan's old VHS tapes I used to always watch. There were Gaither Gospel tapes, a couple of workout tapes Nathan bought because there were women wearing bikinis on the cover, and there was an old Johnny Cash tape I always watched on Sundays after dinner. Then we walked through the house to the back. The roof was caving in near the bathroom. There was a hole in the floor in the back porch. We walked out into the backyard where the Johnny house was. I showed her the field where all of the children used to work. Then we heard this squealing.

"What the fuck is that," Charity said and grabbed my arm. Then she pointed to this possum struggling to walk towards us. It struggled to walk by the tree, but then it fell over, and then it tried to get up again. It looked bloody and there was a sore or a hole in its side where it looked like it had been shot.

"Is it hurt? What's wrong with it?" Charity asked.

I walked closer to it and looked at it. It wasn't playing possum.

"Be careful, Scott," Charity whined.

"It's rabid," I said. I circled around and it stared up at me with its tiny, little eyes. I told her it was the strangest thing, but they always come around people when they got to this point. I told her it probably smelled us out here and came running.

"Why would it do that? Why would they want to come around people?"

It flipped and flopped on the ground and tried to walk. There were blood streaks running through its white hair. Then it tried to walk through a hole in a rusty chain-linked fence and got caught. The jagged fence cut and sliced at its skin. It still tried to pull free, but the fence had it now. It was caught in the fence and it was dying.

Then I heard my Uncle Nathan giggling like a demon from somewhere in the dark.

SO I WENT AWAY

I went away from this place and I lived somewhere else. Years passed. When I came back, it was all the same. It had been years, but the place was the same. I started teaching at the school I went to as a boy. It was a substitute gig. The original teacher needed surgery and she would be out for three weeks. There was a little girl there in the 5th grade class and she was so shy she could barely speak. The other 5th grade teacher told me that the little girl's mother was on drugs. She told me not to get close to the kids like that because they never made it through the school year. They always ended up moving or just disappearing. She told me that she had been to a funeral just a few weeks earlier for a student's mother who had overdosed.

I discovered a few days into teaching that the little girl couldn't read. I stayed after school and tried to teach her. I told myself I was helping her, but who knows. Then I went home in the evenings and waited for the next day to come.

I tried looking for Bill, but I couldn't find him. I asked around but nobody seemed to know. I drove by Ruby's a time or two, but the house was falling in now and it usually just made me sad.

Then one morning I opened up the local paper and read about a robbery and a murder in the Rupert area of an old woman and her husband. There were two pictures of the suspects they had recently arrested. They were kids I knew from long ago. One was Naked Joe who I last saw a year after high school sitting on top of the monkey bars and shooting a pellet gun at some little kids playing nearby. And then there was this other guy who looked different. He had long red hair over his shoulders and a tattoo on his neck. His hair was long and flowing like a lion's mane almost. It was so long and curling and flowing you could barely see his face behind the thick red beard. The beard covered his entire face. He looked like somebody from another world. At first I didn't recognize him but then I saw the name beneath the photo. It was Bill. "Holy shit," I said looking at his long long hair.

He was the little boy who had lice. He was the little boy who collected troll dolls. He was the little boy who decided to fall in love. He was the little boy who dreamed of crossing oceans and the elevations of mountaintops.

I found out what happened just a couple of days later. One Thursday I had stayed after school to help the little girl with her reading, and then afterwards I stopped at a gas station to fill up the car. I was just about finished pumping the gas when I looked at the pump across from me and I saw him. It was Lee Brown. He was still a giant, except he was wearing a shirt and a tie. We both laughed and finished pumping our gas. Then we shook hands. He told me his father was sick and he had come down to see him. He said his father was dying. Lee was a surgeon now (two years out of his residency) and he worked in the emergency room at a hospital in Charleston. He lived two hours away.

The first thing he asked me after we finished catching up was if I heard what happened to Bill. I told him I had but I didn't really know any details. And so he told me. He told me Bill and Joe were into some bad stuff. He told me about how they broke into this house to steal some shit. Bill did the breaking in and Joe did the lookout from the road. They were looking for pills. So Bill was going through the house looking for the bathroom. And then the old lady woke up and she heard him. Lee said her husband was sick and blind and on his deathbed. They broke into their house because they knew he was dying and had pain-killers. And so she came out crying: "My husband's sick. My husband's sick. Please don't take his medicine. Please don't take anything." Then Lee said Bill stole some cheap jewelry, some pills, and some chewing gum.

I said: "What?"

Lee said: "Oh yeah, Lil Bill had four packages of chewing gum that he admitted to stealing when they caught him. He wouldn't admit to the pills or the jewelry though." I just shook my head and listened to the rest of it. I listened to how Bill freaked out and picked up a block of wood sitting next to the stove and then he hit the old woman with it.

And then he hit her again.

And then he hit her again.

Then Lee told me that that wasn't the end of it. He told me that the dying husband came out all blind as shit with a shotgun. He was blind but he was firing the shotgun all over the place. Then Bill and Joe finally took off. Then Lee said that when the ambulance showed up the old man ended up having a heart attack and dying right there—so Bill and Joe were stuck with two murders instead of just one. Lee told me it was called the felony murder rule.

I asked Lee who the old lady was. Lee told me it was the

old junior high math teacher Mrs. Powell. Lee said it was just a coincidence.

I tried forgetting about it. A few weeks later I was after school helping the little girl who couldn't read. Some days it felt like we were making progress, but then the next day we were right back to where we started. I only had a few more days left of substituting before their original teacher came back. I was going to be out of a job soon, and I didn't know what to do.

I was sitting beside the little girl and listening to her read out loud. Every time she came to a difficult word, I asked her to take her time and think about how it would sound, and then say it. She read one word and then she came to a word she didn't know. I noticed every time she came to a difficult word, she would reach into her jacket pocket and pull out a little golden locket on a little golden chain. Then she would speak the word. So she read and she read. She came to a difficult word and she touched the locket. She read the difficult word. She read and she read. She came to a difficult word and she touched the locket. After we were finished, and I was picking up my things, she came to my desk and thanked me for helping her. Then her eyes became teary and she said she had something to tell me.

She said: "I think you know my mother's boyfriend. He did a really bad thing. He's in jail. My mother said the two of you used to live together. She said the two of you were friends a long time ago."

The little girl who didn't know how to read was quiet for a second and she said that she wanted to tell me something else. She said that her mother's boyfriend gave her something the morning of his arrest.

She told me she thought it was beautiful, but she didn't need it if it belonged to the woman who was killed. She said she was sorry for the little old woman and the little old man who died. She told me that her mother's boyfriend had given her a pack of chewing gum too, but she had already chewed it and now it was all gone.

So she took her little fifth-grader hand and reached into her pocket and then she pulled out the golden locket and the golden chain. Then she put it on my desk. I turned the trinket over and it had initials on it. They were Mrs. Powell's initials. They were the initials that belonged to the murdered woman.

I looked at the little girl who looked at me with her green eyes. She was wondering if this was the locket of a dead woman. I thought for a while and touched the locket that belonged to the murder victim. I was about ready to say something when I stopped.

I looked at the locket again and then I told her: "No, this couldn't have belonged to the woman. I know for sure. You just keep it." Then I handed it back to the little girl. And the little girl went back to her desk and got ready to leave. She put the locket on because this wasn't the possession of an old woman who had been murdered, but this was the thing that her mother's boyfriend had given to her. This was the sweet thing that made her feel loved, and this was a chain that made her feel beautiful. This was a golden thing that made her feel like a movie star.

A SHORT HISTORY OF CRAPALACHIA PT 3

So I went home that night and I did something strange. I went through my old books and I picked one out from long ago. I opened it up and I read about Buffalo Creek.

It was February. It was morning. It was 1972. The Pittston Coal Company built a sludge dam on the side of a mountain above a mountain town. I read about how they built the dam to keep it full of toxic coal refuse. This refuse was like muddy black water, thick as oatmeal. One morning the dam broke and the water went rushing down into the valley.

I read about how the disaster killed 125 people. I read about how parents tried to save their children. One father was putting his children on top of their house. He was trying to put his wife up there too, but then the house broke apart like toothpicks. They were all hanging onto their father and being washed away in this giant muddy river. Then a car came barreling towards them in the flood water and knocked into their father. He lost his grip on their mother. The children were still hanging onto him. He was able to swim to safety and put the children on a bank. The last time they saw their mother she was floating down the river and screaming for help. They were their own mother now.

I read about roadways being washed away. I read about people seeing train tracks bent and wrapped around oak trees, coal train cars lifted on top of trees.

I read about how the survivors described it as a giant thirty-foot wave of water.

I read about bodies in trees. I read about the body of a young boy in a tree thirty feet above the ground. He had his hands up in front of his face like he was trying to protect himself.

I read about another body of an old man. There was a dog beside him. The man was dead but the dog wasn't. The dog was protecting the body of the old man. It growled and bit at any rescue worker who tried to get close. The dog did this for days.

I read about how they didn't find people with injuries. They found only people who were dead or ones who were left without a scratch. One house was destroyed and the house beside it was still standing with the car left untouched in the gravel driveway.

I read about the rescue workers using a bulldozer to push through the mud. They found an artificial leg, but they didn't find the person who the artificial leg belonged to. They came across all of these baby dolls with their little baby doll hands reaching out of the mud. The rescue worker pulled out one baby doll by its hand. They freed it. Then he pulled out another baby doll hand. They freed it. Then they saw another little baby doll hand and pulled at it. It wasn't a baby doll hand. It was the hand of a five-year-old girl. She had already been dressed that morning. She wasn't in her pajamas. She was wearing a pink dress.

They cleaned her up and tried to comb her muddy hair and put her in a body bag.

Three days later they found the body of a woman sitting against a tree. I read about how the rescue workers couldn't believe they had not found her earlier. They had walked past her body perhaps hundreds of times. How could that be? They even ate lunch beside that tree one day and still didn't see her. She was sitting against the tree and looking out at the river and she was dead. There was some sand in her mouth, but her body was untouched. There were no bruises. There were no broken bones. There were no gashes on her head.

I read about how two days later the rescue workers were walking past a row of caskets in the morgue. They looked inside one casket and there was the little girl in the pink. And in the same coffin right beside the little girl was the woman they found sitting against a tree. They didn't know that these bodies found days apart were more than just bodies. The woman sitting against the tree was a mother. The little girl in the pink dress was her daughter.

I read about how the Pittston Coal Company said it was an act of God.

Then I looked up from the book and put it away. I saw all of the people I had known and loved being washed away in that flood. I saw Ruby and Nathan. I saw Stanley and Mary. I saw my uncles and my aunts and all the McClanahans. I saw Bill and his family. I saw Lee and all the crazy fuckers. I saw Sarah. They were all being washed away and they were all doing something else. They were all screaming.

AND NOW...

My water keeps rising. My water keeps rolling.

SO I FAILED

My home was gone. So I decided to write this book. I tried to remember all of the people and phantoms I had ever known and loved. I tried to make them laugh and dance, move and dream, love and see. I put some of them together and twisted our time together. I tried to bring them back, but I couldn't. I started digging on the mountain years ago. I pushed the shovel down deep into the rocky ground and I cut out clumps of dirt and stones hard as gall.

My wife even asked me one morning, "What the hell are you doing."

I didn't say anything to her, but I took the dirt and stones and I put them in plastic bags. Then I traveled. I went to Pittsburgh, PA, and Chicago, IL, and Atlanta, GA. I went back to Pittsburgh, PA. I left my dirt there in the streets. I went back to Chicago, IL. I went to New York City. I went to Washington, DC. I went to Charlotte, NC. I went to Raleigh, NC. I went to Oxford, MS. I went to Ann Arbor, MI—the home of Iggy Pop and the ever beautiful Elizabeth Ellen. I went to Portland, OR. I dreamed of China. I dreamed of India, Berlin, Paris, London. I went to Seattle, WA. I went to New York City and I dropped my dirt.

I went to New York City. I went to New York City for a third time. I went to New York City.

I gave my dirt away to the people I met. I called it magic dirt and they laughed. They put it in flower pots and the flowers grew. I dropped the stones on the sidewalks. I told them I was going to make the whole world Crapalachia, but they didn't believe me. They thought I was only joking. I think of Sarah asking me why I was doing this.

I told her I was putting blankets in the trees for our children, so that no matter where they went—they would always be home. The whole world would become this place. It would take a million years and it would take a million trips, but I would rearrange the world.

She said, "That's impossible, Scott, and it's also crazy."

I told her that's why I needed to do it. I told her that was the only reason to do anything.

So now I put the dirt from my home in my pockets and I travel. I am making the world my mountain.

So we have to come to the end. Listen: Your heart is beating. Isn't that amazing? Your heart believes in you. I believe in your heart too.

I wanted to write a book about all the people I knew and loved before I forgot them, but I see that my book is something else now. I see that I have been praying a selfish prayer for myself. I see that I have been praying this prayer…

Please tell me I existed. Please tell me I was born. Please tell me I sang,

and laughed, and danced, and saw and dreamed. I am beyond fucking
memories now. It is a time for forgetting. ~~God bless the forgotten. God bless~~
~~the forgetful.~~

We pass the torch of life for one another like runners in the
night. I WILL forever be reaching for you. PLEASE keep reaching for me. Please.

APPENDIX AND NOTES

I am going to start this appendix with an observation...
How do you know England is an island? Have you ever walked
around its borders? How do you know this appendix is true? Is
it because I told you so?

Actually there were only 12 of them. I've always said there
were 13 of them because I was told once that Ruby lost two
babies rather than one. It always felt better when I said 13 anyway. So really there were only 11 of them because I know for
sure Ruby had a baby who died before Stirley was born. My
Aunt Annie got married when she was young and moved away.
She was the oldest, so really it was like there were only 10 of
them. Grover moved away as well. By the time my dad was born,
it was like there were only 9 or 8 or 7 of them.

Out of the 11 children, 5 of them committed suicide. It could
have been six. It could have been four. My dad doesn't know for
sure. He said he would have to check. He said he wasn't really
sure how many children there even were in Elgie's family. Elgie's
mother died when he was young so no one ever talked about it.

I told my dad that once four children commit suicide what does it really matter if it's five or six or four? Who knows?

I have never had a million babies explode from my smile and start running all over the world. I am looking forward to that day though.

For some reason I decided to call my father Uncle Stanley in this book. I was tired of writing about my mom and dad in the books *Stories, Stories II, Stories V!* and *Hill William.* So whenever my Uncle Stanley says something in this book (minus his comment about homosexual marriage and the word *sheeeeett*) it is actually my father who is speaking in real life.

It was around the time of Ruby's mastectomy that I found out that Ziggy Stardust and the Spiders from Mars weren't really from Mars. I was further shocked when I found out that Ziggy Stardust was actually a man named David Bowie. I was even more shocked when I found out David Bowie's real name was David Jones, but he changed it for commercial reasons. There was already a singer who was using the name Davy Jones.

I've been thinking about the story of the little girl getting her toes cut off all weekend, and I'm not sure if it was plural *toes.* I keep thinking that maybe it was only a big toe.

I never actually lived with Ruby and Nathan. I only stayed with them for extended periods of time. I was at Ruby's at least two or three days every week of my entire life. Two of my earliest memories are playing in Ruby's apple trees and her putting Vicks salve on my chest. I remember the way her bedspread felt on my soft skin when I slept with her at night. I never actually intentionally define whether I lived with Ruby and Nathan, but many people have assumed this was the case. What may have felt like vague family parameters is actually nothing more than the "crapalachian/scot/irish" concept of the extended family.

I never poured beer down Nathan's feeding tube. Ruby wouldn't have stood for that. There was less freedom for Nathan than what was in this book. However, he constantly begged me to bring him a six-pack. He would do this as a joke and sometimes he wouldn't. When Rhonda gave him Ensure he used to tell us it was a six-pack. I let him drink the beer in this book because I wanted to give him a chance to be free for a moment. I wanted to give him a chance to enjoy something. This is the truth of my Nathan.

The line of dialogue about Ruby telling me not to eat the gallstones was never said by Ruby. She did have her gallbladder removed but she never said this line of dialogue. I created it from a story that concerned my Aunt Bernice and my Uncle Leslie. My Aunt Bernice had her gallbladder removed as well. When Bernice awoke from the anesthesia my Uncle Leslie came into the room. The doctor had put her gallstones in an orange pill bottle on the table beside her bed. My Uncle Leslie tried to make Bernice take them because he thought they were medicine. My Aunt Bernice said, "That's not my medicine. Those are my gallstones."

In the last few years of Ruby's life my dad and the other brothers had a falling out with my Uncle Stanley over some borrowed money. My Uncle Leslie went over to Stanley's house to ask for the borrowed money back. He took off his boots. Stanley threatened to kick his ass. My dad said Leslie deserved to get his ass kicked if he took his boots off before asking for the money.

I called my dad Uncle Stanley because I wanted to bring

Stanley back into the family. I wanted to put the family back together again. I wanted to call the prodigal son home. I wanted to make him someone important in this book. So I took what my father said and did, and I said my Uncle Stanley said and did it. I made him my father. I made them one. I heard Stanley had a heart attack last year. When a family is cut open—this is what happens. People you loved, people whose houses you've stayed in, people who you have known forever, become strangers to you. They have heart attacks and you don't even call. You don't even remember. My Uncle Stanley was the first man to take me fishing. My Uncle Stanley was the first man I saw drink a beer without shame. He didn't hide it. My Uncle Stanley was the first man who fed me pizza when I was a baby.

My mother said this to me the other night. "Why are you calling this book *Crapalachia*? That's not a good title. It's a horrible title." I told her, "No it's not. It's a good title. Shit makes the flowers grow."

I wanted to put the story of John Henry in this book, but I left it out for some reason. John Henry battled the steam engine. The town of Talcott, West Virginia, claims this battle happened there. Did it really? In my dreams it did. God bless the myths of this world. God bless those who keep trying to make myths. It's all we have.

Actually Rhonda is the one who took the pictures of the dead faces to Rite Aid. There is no way you could walk to Rite Aid. You had to drive. Rite Aid was twenty miles from Ruby's house. I had the conversation with her about the pictures though.

Little Bill's lice actually happened in the 3rd grade, not junior high.

Mrs. Powell wasn't the junior high math teacher. Mrs. Powell was actually our 3rd grade teacher. I wanted to put her name in this book so that her generations will know how nervous she made me feel.

I never sent a letter for Nathan. I did write one though, but I wrote it on behalf of myself. "I wrote a love letter for a girl once. I gave it to her and later that day I overheard her making fun of me. I overheard her making fun of my love." I just heard that line in a movie I'm watching, so I wrote it down and decided to put it in my book. I wanted this moment of watching a movie to last too.

The character of Little Bill is made up of two people. It is a composite character. The first part of the character is made up of a school friend of mine whose name was Bill Terry. The second part of his character is made of a person named Phil Crookshanks. They were my friends. I knew them. Why did I do this? I'm getting older. It seems like all of my friends from long ago are slowly becoming one friend. Even now I actually have trouble keeping them apart. Bill was the one who had lice. Bill was the one who murdered. Phil was the one who couldn't stop thinking the bad thoughts and who loved the beautiful Janette. Phil was the one I lived with.

There were things I didn't write about Phil. I didn't write about not having any money and asking Phil to drive me to the mall. It was December and the mall was far away. It was snowing but we took off in the late afternoon. We listened to Queen. We ordered our Chick-fil-A with our pennies. We sat and ate it and it tasted wonderful. It tasted like we would never be hungry again. Freddie Mercury is still amazing.

There is another story I didn't write about Phil because it

would make me look bad. This is one of the things I'm ashamed of. We were in high school and I saw him at one of the football games. I was hanging out with these two girls. We'd just come back from the woods and we were drinking whiskey out of a plastic Mountain Dew bottle. I was with two girls and I said, "You know what? You look like a Cro-Magnon man."

A few years later I was drinking brandy in our room. We were roommates now. I was with two girlfriends again. I was laughing and having a good time being drunk. One of the girls wanted to leave because I kept kissing her friend and she kept kissing me back. Then Bill turned to me and there were tears in his eyes. He said, "So you think I look like a Cro-Magnon man, huh?" He started crying when he said it. It had been years but he was still hurt by it. I didn't know what he meant for a few moments. I had forgotten, but he remembered. One day I will pay for these things.

So I took these shadows of my friends and placed them together. The generations are becoming one.

I actually worry I should change the names of the real people in this book. I worry they will track me down and kill me. That's the problem with telling the truth. That's the only thing I'm worried about, a beating. I'll get it one day. That's a fact. Maybe.

You can find re-runs of *Walker, Texas Ranger* on many channels. Check your local listings. It's the best piece of art you'll ever find. If you can watch it without irony, you'll understand Nathan. It's not a comedy. Remember that.

Nathan tried to take his life years earlier, not before his death. It was the early '80s and I was a child, but it happened this way. I put the way he tried to take his life in the middle of the Rhonda story.

Nathan McClanahan, Elgie McClanahan, and Ruby McClanahan are buried on Backus Mountain near Layland, WV. Their graves are waiting for flowers. I haven't visited them in years.

This book should not be thought of or included in a genre of literature called the Appalachian Minstrel Show. The names of writers who have written in this genre include Lee Smith, Mary Lee Settle, Silas House, and a list that goes on and on. They know who they are.

The recipe in this book is not Ruby's recipe. Ruby didn't use recipes. This is a recipe I googled. My wife said, "What is the problem with these women? They never write anything down." You had to watch them to know. You had to be there to learn. If you cook this recipe you will be bringing someone else to life. Ruby's cooking is forever lost to my generations.

I stole the title of the chapter YOU CAN'T PUT YOUR ARMS AROUND A RECIPE from a Johnny Thunders song. I changed the word *memory* to *recipe*.

The line about the crazy ass rivers means the Tigris and Euphrates. Our whole entire fucked up world is because of geography.

I just realized that I never look at a painting and ask, "Is this painting fictional or non-fictional?" It's just a painting.

I didn't live with Bill during high school. I lived with my mom and dad. I lived with Bill (Phil) years afterwards. Actually my grandmother died after I lived with Bill. I lived with Bill at college, but college never appears in Appalachian books. We can't admit these sorts of things. We can't admit we've gone to malls. We can't admit we've gone to restaurants. We can't admit we dream our dreams. People won't believe you.

The days are correct on Nathan's funeral notice, but the years aren't.

I'm not sure why I keep talking about skipping school. We went to school all of the time. I bought a book on film at a yard sale. It was published in the mid-sixties. I read about *The 400 Blows* and I wanted to be a bad kid. I wanted to skip school and escape from reformatories. I read Huck Finn. I wanted to be a runaway. I wasn't running. I was a good kid. I listened to my parents. I loved them. I didn't want to disappoint them. I didn't want to break their hearts. I still feel like lighting out for the territories.

Dr. Mustafa Mahboob is still in Beckley. He is still accepting patients. You can look him up in the phone book and set up an appointment for psychiatric help today. It might make you feel better to talk to someone.

Lee Brown. I cut a couple of Lee Brown stories out of this book, but I want to put them back in. I won't though. If you ever meet me, just ask me about them and I will tell you. I want him to be remembered.

Pit Row wasn't below the apartment. We couldn't look down from the window and see Pit Row. I've told the story this way for so long that I can't move it back. Stories can actually rearrange continents if they're told long enough. It's actually in the Bible. Matthew 15:6-7 states, "If you only had the faith of mustard seeds and stories—we could move mountains and the location of gas stations."

For actual cassette tapes of these prank phone call conversations—you should contact Sergeant First Class Charles Wayne Tiller at his air force base in Oklahoma City, Oklahoma. As teenagers we taped them and he still has the cassette tapes. The last time I listened to one was about five years ago. We also have a prank phone call we made to Jim Leyland and Tommy Lasorda. If you called the Pirates ticket line 1-800-Go-Bucs and let it ring through without choosing any option, an operator would pick up. You simply had to say "clubhouse" and the telephone would ring into the managerial offices. Tommy Lasorda actually called Reinaldo a faggot. Tommy Lasorda was an obvious homophobe.

I wasn't in high school when the Sago Mine disaster happened. I graduated high school in 1996. This happened years later. When this happened, I was living in the house I live in now. I was watching college football bowl games that entire week.

I wouldn't put midget the dog on the list of things I've loved anymore. I really hated that fucking dog. I wouldn't put Arlene Maguire or Tom Maguire into this list either. I understand why you divorced one another.

The police never questioned me. I was in the 9th grade when the school break-in happened. Besides, I never lived with Bill Terry. I lived with Phil Crookshanks. Bill Terry was the one who broke into the school with this kid named Alvin. No one knows who truly took a shit in the principal's desk.

For the specifics of the murder you should see *The State of West Virginia vs. Bill Terry*. It should be on file in the Greenbrier County, WV, courthouse. If you have LexisNexis, I'm sure you can find it. Bill Terry was a good kid. He was shy. I've never met someone so shy. He had the blondest hair of any of my friends.

Once again, Mrs. Powell should have been nicer to her students and I wouldn't have allowed her to be murdered in this book.

I was a substitute teacher at the school where my mother taught. My mom was a teacher. This happened to my mother, but I was standing there when it happened. The little girl didn't show her a locket. The little girl showed her a pile of baseball cards and a cheap necklace. There were no initials, but the little girl was worried they belonged to the old woman Bill may have murdered. I told her to keep them, and then my mother agreed.

The last line about passing the torch of life is stolen from the poet Lucretius. He has been dead for years but he is still alive.

I have written this book in four different ways now. The first time I wrote this book was in the year 2000. I wrote a book called *Grandma Ruby's*. In 2004 I wrote a book called *Phil Crookshanks*. In 2006 I wrote a book full of short stories I broke apart from the original book called *Phil Crookshanks*. In the year 2011 I cut all of these books apart and put them together into one book called *Crapalachia*. I want to thank this book for being my friend. I will miss being a part of this book. I will miss remembering these people.

I wrote this appendix during the last week of Sarah's pregnancy. I ate Kentucky Fried Chicken on the day I finished it. I typed it up on the day of my son's birth, April 19, 2012. Today is April 21st. Yesterday, Iris gave Samuel a kiss when he came home from the hospital. My wife is asleep upstairs with the oldest child. My mother-in-law is awake with Samuel. They are upstairs too. We are all trying to sleep. I am forever trying to sleep.

This book is a time machine. The words you have just read are the past. The next page is the future. Your beautiful, young bodies and your beautiful, young faces are the present.

The PRESENT...

Enjoy it while it fucking lasts.

I want to thank you for your time, even though time doesn't belong to you either.

So farewell my old friends. Farewell.

Also published by **TWO DOLLAR RADIO**

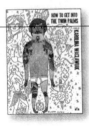

HOW TO GET INTO THE TWIN PALMS

A NOVEL BY KAROLINA WACLAWIAK

A Trade Paperback Original; 978-0-9832471-8-0; $16 US

"One of my favorite books this year." —*The Rumpus*

"Waclawiak's novel reinvents the immigration story."
—*New York Times Book Review, Editors' Choice*

RADIO IRIS

A NOVEL BY ANNE-MARIE KINNEY
A Trade Paperback Original; 978-0-9832471-7-3; $16 US

"Kinney is a Southern California Camus." —*Los Angeles Magazine*

"[*Radio Iris*] has a dramatic otherworldly payoff that is unexpected and triumphant."
—*New York Times Book Review, Editors' Choice*

THE PEOPLE WHO WATCHED HER PASS BY

A NOVEL BY SCOTT BRADFIELD
A Trade Paperback Original; 978-0-9820151-5-5; $14.50 US

"Challenging [and] original... A billowy adventure of a book. In a book
that supplies few answers, Bradfield's lavish eloquence is the presiding
constant."
—*New York Times Book Review*

FREQUENCIES

A new non-fiction journal of artful essays!

"The quality of each piece makes this journal heavy with literary weight."
—*NewPages*

VOLUME 1 / FALL 2012, NOW AVAILABLE! $10 U.S.; 978-1-937512-01-9
Essays by Blake Butler, Joshua Cohen, Tracy Rose Keaton, Scott McClanahan;
Interview with Anne Carson.

VOLUME 2 / SPRING 2013, COMING SOON! $10 U.S.; 978-1-937512-08-8
Essays by Sara Finnerty, Roxane Gay, Alex Jung, Aaron Shulman, Kate Zambreno; and more!

FREQUENCIES *annual subscriptions available for $15 at* __TwoDollarRadio.com!__